Openings

Openings

A Zen Joke Guide for Serious Problem Solving

George A. Katchmer, Jr.

YMAA Publication Center
Jamaica Plain, Mass. USA

Publisher's Cataloging in Publication
(Prepared by Quality Books Inc.)

Katchmer, George A., 1948-
    Openings : a Zen joke guide for serious problem solving / by
George A. Katchmer, Jr.
    p. cm.
    ISBN: 1-886969-45-0

    1. Self-actualization (Psychology) 2. Self-realization. 3. Problem solv-
ing--Problems, exercises, etc. 4. Sucess in business. I. Title.

BF637.S4K38 1996   158.1
                              QBI96-20362

Copyright ©1996 by George A. Katchmer, Jr.

First Printing 1996
3

ISBN 1-886969-45-0
Printed in Canada

YMAA Publication Center   楊氏武藝協會

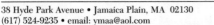
38 Hyde Park Avenue • Jamaica Plain, MA 02130
(617) 524-9235 • email: ymaa@aol.com

Foreword

After reading *Openings* I was convinced that many of life's problems are as big or as little as we want to make them. George A. Katchmer's stories paint vivid pictures of life's complexities, and tell how to survive in an increasingly complicated world. He emphasizes the need to rely on all of our potential as human beings—the rational and the non-rational. According to Katchmer, we all have immense creative and intuitive abilities, and he shows us how to apply these abilities to the numerous issues confronting us every day. His humor and wit are delightful and make for very easy and enjoyable reading.

I have worked with various groups on developing and utilizing intuition, and I am not at all surprised to see that some of the same concepts are being offered by business consultants, educational institutions, and now a Buddhist prosecuting attorney in Ohio. *Openings* demonstrates the value of our intuitive abilities and teaches us how to develop and utilize them for our advantage.

The pendulum is swinging away from a strictly scientific paradigm and towards a more integrated approach to living, an approach that encompasses what we feel as well as what we can rationally prove. If you are happy with the results you get from doing the exercises described in this book, does it really matter if the methods stand up to "scientific" scrutiny?

George Katchmer does a great job of showing us non-traditional ways of dealing with common problems. It's nice to know that logic isn't the only, or even the best approach to solving a problem, but simply one of many tools that each of us have at our disposal.

Jeffrey S. Blanck is an attorney, a board member of the International Alliance of Holistic Lawyers, a member of the Intuitive Bar Association, and Vice President in charge of Administration of TMI, a management consulting and training company in San Rafael, California.

Introduction

We've all been between a rock and a hard place. Most of us probably figure that we spend the bulk of our time there. We know how it *feels*. Unfortunately, most of us don't trust our feelings so we tend to get eaten alive by our problems. This, I am convinced, is because we have been erroneously taught that all problems are basically rational things that have, somewhere, somehow, a corresponding rational solution. It will come as quite a shock to you then that this book stands for the proposition that no problems are rational—let me make this clear—not most problems, not some problems, not a few problems, but no problems are inherently rational. After all, if the world were an entirely rational place, there could be no problems. This book stands for the further corollary that since all problems are irrational in nature, the only possible solutions can themselves, be inherently and blissfully irrational.

If you doubt me, or think that what I am stating here is nonsense, then, Mr. Spock, I am fully prepared to pull rank on you. I'll prove my proposition logically. Don't let this excursion into analytical philosophy put you off, but logical statements are logical statements simply because and by definition, they *already* imply and fully and totally include every true proposition that can be derived from them. There are no surprises in logic. They are ruled out by definition. Hence, no surprises, no problems. If you don't believe me on this, consult the works of Ludwig Wittgenstein, Bertrand Russell, or, if you are really anal about it, Immanuel Kant.

But enough of dead Germans and dead Englishmen. Since there are problems in the world, the world is bloated with irrationality. And that, my friend, is precisely what I wish in this book to teach you. How to think and act irrationally. Now, I didn't say to act crazy. I said irrationally. There is a difference.

Carl Jung theorized that the human mind or psyche survives by adapting itself to its environment. It does this by means of four antennae that it pokes out into its world like an amoeba does with its pseudopodia. These four antennae are what Jung calls the psyche's four functions. They are: thinking, sensation, feeling, and intuition. We use them to learn about our world and adapt where necessary in order to survive. Sensation and thinking Jung termed the "rational" functions; feeling and intuition are the "irrational" functions. While none is superior to the others, in the West we have been taught to value only the so-called "rational" functions. This is unfortunate, not because these rational functions are unimportant, but because the exclusion of the other functions from our lives forces us to face the world dressed in our pin-striped suit—minus our pants. We are half-dressed and half-prepared. I hope to remedy that by providing you with methods whereby you can contact your irrational mind and let it help you solve the most pressing problems in your lives—and I'll wager, the most pervasive ones—those that apparently have no rational solution. The unsolvable problem.

I used the term "method" above. I guess that term is as appropriate in this context as the idea that Zen Buddhism is a "method." My exercises will work for you. I know that for a fact. However, none of them are chipped in stone and none of them have any meaning whatsoever if they do not have meaning to you personally and individually.

There are serious problems, very serious problems, and then, in a galaxy of the highest magnitude, are the problems that affect you personally.

I had a close friend during the 1960s when I went to college who found that by doing certain things to his body, he could end up in the emergency room. As my friend sat waiting for his intern to return, watching the wallpaper do things that the manufacturer never intended, he was struck by a sudden Zen-like insight: "This is important, this is me!"

All problems are ultimately personal. They are important because they are you. Only you can approach, define, and handle your own problems. Take what I say on these pages as a joke. It is a joke, however, that we share. If we laugh together it means that you know how to laugh. If you can laugh, you are using the irrational part of your mind. Perhaps, in the end, it is the ultimate rationality.

The first chapter deals with the nature of human life and the gaps in rationality inherent in it. The second chapter describes the power that one has by framing questions—by controlling the energy of your problem. Chapter 3 gives various methods and processes for reaching a solution to the most difficult types of problems: The Nebulous Problem and the Booby Trap.

Chapter 4 expands on the methodology of chapter 3 and helps us to "capture" a problem by baiting it with analogy. Chapter 5 teaches us how to "act" on a problem, which is the only real solution, and, finally, chapter 6 shows you your enemies, very much as Alexander did when he kicked the bodies of slain Persian soldiers on the battlefield to show his men that the feared Persians, too, were just as liable as anyone else to die. They had no magic power. Neither do your worst fears and greatest worries.

I called this book *Openings*, following the Buddhist way of looking at the world. The world consists of atoms of experience called *dharmas* and large open spaces. It is these open spaces that we wish to occupy and fill so that we may tap their energy and solve our problems. Now let's go poke fun at some monsters together.

CHAPTER ONE | # Poking Holes in Your Life

I grew up during the 1950s. This fact usually scares people. Actually, I mean that it scares most of the people I work with these days since most of them are younger than me. I'm a lawyer, a prosecutor to be exact. During the fifties, the time in which my tender sensibilities were formed, lawyers looked like Spencer Tracy or Raymond Burr, or, if one were a little more progressive, Paul Newman in *The Young Philadelphians.* Later, in the sixties, lawyers would begin to look like Gregory Peck in *To Kill a Mockingbird* and then Paul Newman again in *The Verdict,* ending with a pony-tailed, dope-smoking James Wood in *True Believer.* We've come a long way, baby.

At any rate, the lawyers I deal with weren't even born until the year I graduated from high school. They have no sense of history. They can't remember a time before TV, a time before snack trays, and, heaven forbid, a time before indoor plumbing. I do. Excuse me, I need a drink.

The fifties sit like this dark mist prior to most of my colleagues' frames of reference. Dragons, newts, basilisks, etc., are known and scientifically proven to have walked the earth at that time. It was a time of heroes and legends.

By the mid-fifties, I was one of the first generation of TV

zombies. The programming got better, as Disney flooded the airwaves with a variety of shows—"The Mickey Mouse Club," "Davy Crockett," and a collection of second-string Crocketts—all with lucrative commercial tie-ins such as coonskin caps, etc. The grass has never been known to grow under Mickey's oversized foot.

Friday nights were the focal point of the TV week for all of us little munchkins. No school on Saturday. Party time. Popcorn, pizzas, and root-beer—the good kind, 29 cents a quart and all sugar—for everyone.

My father was a football coach at the local college and would spend Friday nights with his team sacrificing virgins, reading the entrails of bats, and other arcane football things. This meant that my mother was in charge of four kids. Her strategy was that if we were hypnotized by TV and our hands were full of pizza and root-beer, she was safe.

One of the Disney "classics" appearing on Friday nights, and a favorite of mine, was "Zorro." And "Zorro" is as good a place as any for us to jump off into our discussion of dealing with unsolvable problems.

Imagine, here is young Don Diego de la Vega, handsome (with a mustache, he was Spanish, after all, and we all know that every Spanish man, every single one of them, sports a mustache) and the greatest swordsman in Spain. Not just California mind you, but in the real place, Spain.

Don Diego is actually from the sleepy little mission hamlet of Los Angeles. When we first see him he is in Spain saying goodbye to his friends, the senoritas, and skewering one last soul for old times sake. His father, Don Alejandro, has called him home. Madrid will never be the same. Women fan themselves in frustration, men wipe their brows and begin to openly wear their swords again.

Meanwhile, in Los Angeles, aforementioned sleepy mission hamlet, the freedom and, one must not neglect, financial security of the *rancheros* is being threatened by the evil grip of the evil commandante, Capitan Monastario (For those who doubt the power of television, explain to me how, as a 47 year-old man in a semi-responsible position, I can remember the name of Zorro's commandante?) Commandante Monastario's right-hand man is the bumbling idiot, Sergeant Garcia, a spiritual forerunner of Sergeant Schultz.

As soon as Diego gets off the boat, he gets the score. Pillaging, beatings, soldiers getting all the best women—this had to stop!

Don Deigo, however, is only one man. The greatest swordsman in all of Spain, but one man nonetheless. What could he, as one man do against the entrenched—and legal—power of the commandante and his overwhelming band of soldiers? Here, my friend, is the unsolvable problem.

But Diego was also a cunning blade. He knew that he must strike at night. He knew that he must disguise himself in such a way as to strike fear into the hearts of the evildoers, so, the black-caped crusader—I've heard this before—Zorro was born.

Zorro was quite effective, stealing the commandante's gold, embarrassing him in front of the senoritas, and giving hope to the good patrons and peons in Old Los Angeles.

In order to do his good deeds however, Don Diego could not let anyone suspect that he was in fact, Zorro. The commandante, after all, was not a complete idiot, he would simply burn the Vega hacienda, throw everyone into jail, and hunt Don Diego like a dog.

So Don Diego, the greatest swordsman in Spain, solved his problem by becoming a new person—Don Diego de la Vega, effeminate fop and amateur minstrel. He sported pastel clothing, lace sleeve hankies—all of the Leslie Howard paraphernalia that he could muster. He was so effective that his own father was disgusted with him and the evil commandante, El Capitan Monastario found him amusing and invited him to his parties to help entertain the young eligible lovelies of Old L.A.

We all know the rest of the story, of course. He stole Monastario's gold, exposed him to his superiors in Spain, who were naturally motivated by kindness and a sense of justice—just ask the Indians in New Spain—and forced him into retirement on the Costa del Sol where he wrote his memoirs, married an actress from the Madrid stage, and started a lucrative series of motivational lectures that took him in front of the crowned heads of Europe.

Sergeant Garcia got off with only a few pairs of Z-sliced underwear. He is still in the Spanish army as far as we know.

Now in assessing Don Diego, a personal hero of mine, as we will shortly see, one has to recognize that his problem-solving genius rested not in creating Zorro, who, except for the cape, was the real Don Diego, greatest swordsman in Spain, but in creating the fool, Don Diego de la Vega. The creation of the foppish Diego allowed him to mingle in society, gain military intelligence, and totally efface his prior reputation as—the greatest swordsman in Spain.

The impossible problem.

You might well ask what the relevance of the fictional character Zorro is to a contemporary discussion of problem-solving? I'll get personal.

In the Montgomery County Prosecutor's Office, where I was employed until the publication of this book, there is a training pattern for all attorneys entering the office. First is a stint in Support Enforcement where the lucky law school graduate is rewarded for all his or her sweat, sacrifice, and determination by being forced to mingle with the absolute cream of society in attempting to get their recalcitrant mates or rutting partners to actually pay for the offspring they have sired. Sterilization was always a hot topic around the water cooler.

After a year of child support, which is all that the human brain can handle this side of sanity, one is moved into the Criminal Division. Here, one does a half year of preliminary hearings. They get you into court, get you used to the rules of evidence, and have the added feature of counting for absolutely nothing.

Then, and here is where Don Diego will re-enter our narrative, one is posted to grand jury. In grand jury one has, for the first time, real power and the concomitant ability to screw up.

A word about grand juries. While it may not be readily apparent to the man or woman in the street, grand juries, your neighbors, your friends, co-workers, are God. Their sessions are conducted in secret and their decisions, unlike those of any other court, board, or tribunal in this great land, are subject to no second-guessing by any court. Their decisions categorically are unquestionable. Scary, isn't it?

A grand jury in Ohio has eleven to fifteen people on it. Only nine vote at any one time. It takes seven to indict. Indictment puts the indictee into the criminal system, requiring him to get a lawyer and exposing him or her to the full force of the criminal justice system, including trial and possibly prison. Nobody else in this country has the power of a grand juror.

To the grand jury in Ohio are assigned two prosecutors. The duty usually falls on two partially trained, green attorneys. The cops know this and use any trick in the book to fake them out or intimidate them so as to get an indictment. And here lies the problem. Police statistics depend on getting an indictment. The prosecutor's statistics depend on trial wins. Once a cop gets his indictment, he's ready to go on his merry way. "Trial? Why, I'll be fishing in Canada on that date. Can't you make a deal?" Well, no, we can't make a deal because our stats, unlike yours, depend on winning trials at the highest indicted felony level.

See the problem?

Several years ago the grand jury in our county was in disarray, to say the least. Police officers routinely ignored their subpoenas and basically showed up to testify whenever there was a conjunction of Jupiter and Neptune in the third decant of their birth signs, and the attorneys had such little control that the cases eventually reaching the trial attorneys were untriable. The attorneys rebelled. But being county workers, who cared? Then, the grand jury itself walked out. Simply walked out. This got some attention since prosecutors in Ohio are elected. They are politicians.

One of my friends, an ex-Marine captain, was called in to a private meeting with the prosecutor. (Not my present employer, heh-heh.)

"Good morning, Phelps. This is Milos Kronar and Eva Schwartzkopf. They are our current grand jury attorneys. Kronar and Schwartzkopf are unaware that there are now orders to take them out. Your mission, should you decide to accept it, is to take over the grand jury, along with (ta-da!) George Katchmer, and clean it up. Of course, if you are killed or captured, the prosecutor's office will disavow any knowledge of your existence. This tape will self-destruct in five seconds. Good morning Mr. Phelps."

The tape dissolved and Phelps and I found ourselves in grand jury.

Our first task was to get the cops to actually show up. Phelps explained to them that subpoenas were not the same as invitations to the Policeman's Ball and that if they didn't show up when ordered, we would dismiss the case. The first day Phelps did this, an officer whose case had been dismissed made a motion for his holster. Phelps stood his ground. A credit to the Corps, I can personally testify. The cops started honoring their subpoenas.

Next, was the more subtle task of actually having evidence of a crime. We made a simple rule. No evidence, no indictment. The lousy, untriable cases started to dry up. We found that fully forty percent of the cases presented fell into that category. Phelps and I were not very popular at FOP meetings. Most of the blame, however, fell on Phelps. I, being the junior attorney, was assumed to be simply Phelps' dupe.

After a half year of this, Phelps decided to go back to trial work before he was found slumped over a fence on some deserted county road, an obvious suicide. I—lucky me—was left to complete Phelps' work alone.

Phelps' agreement with the head prosecutor was indeed secret. The prosecutor had even neglected to tell his first assistant, my direct boss, Sergeant Garcia.

Because of Phelps and me, the grand jury stats were horrible. We killed (failed to indict) forty percent of the cases. Garcia, being used to the good ol' rubber-stamping procedures of bygone days, started summoning me to his office to rant at me on a regular basis.

I needed some way to keep control of the quality of the grand jury indictments and to avoid a direct order to indict everything that wiggled through the door. It was then that Don Diego de la Vega walked back into my life. I became Don Diego. Who says television is not a learning tool!

In order to preserve the reforms Phelps and I instituted, and which I firmly believe helped assure the integrity of the entire criminal justice system in our community, I became a fool. Whenever Garcia confronted me, I simply played stupid.

"Why wasn't such and such a case indicted?"

"Gee, I don't know, boss. Those people are plumb crazy!"

"Well, why didn't you tell them such and such?"

"Golly, I didn't know I could do that. Shazam!"

I really was not an incompetent buffoon, by the way. Needless to say, I was eventually bumped up to trial work and the Policemen's Ball started up again. Don Diego, however, had bought me, and the people of Montgomery County, six months of unadulterated justice. Once again, he was the solution to an exceedingly tough problem.

To say that we all, everyone, doctors, lawyers, teachers, executives, parents, students, face tough problems is to say nothing at all. Of course we do. Approximately one-quarter of the world's population officially believe that life is suffering. Another quarter finds life itself a "problem," and another decent-sized proportion see it as absurd. Whoever is left curses and drinks a lot which also gives testimony to the obvious fact that life is tough and full of problems.

In answer to this, human beings have religion and anesthetics. We also have a plethora of self-help and get-your-life-in-gear-Spunky type of books, videotapes, lectures, etc. I sincerely hope this book is not simply another of the same.

Let's again turn to the obvious. Your life stinks. Anywhere from cheap perfume to week-old fish. I'll just bet you that if you calm down, stop smoking, exercise, stop drinking, eat better, take vitamins, stop popping off at your spouse, your kids, your boss, and your God, and meditate to New Age music on top of it all, by golly, your life will improve! No fooling!

We are all also cognizant of the fact that this is all fine and dandy until a real problem confronts us. This could be anything from impending death to corporate downsizing to any sort of scurrilous habit your kid may decide to pick up. Now, these problems in themselves are still not unsolvable problems. There are rational steps everyone can follow to face them. Death, for example, is the ultimate. Okay, there are innumerable books on grieving. Your local pastor or psychologist will be glad to listen to you. In fact, in the case of death, time itself is probably the best solution. We live in a society, in short, where "rationality" is the keynote and, where, since there is a study on damn near everything, we are led to believe that if we only follow the technique, voila! our problem, even the most severe, is potentially solvable. Severity does not necessarily mean insolubility.

But is life all that rational? For millennia humankind has supported and pursued the most outrageous of superstitions. Rationality had an uphill struggle and, quite frankly, humankind still does not believe on a gut level that life is in any way rational.

As I have pointed out in my previous books, *The Tao of*

Bioenergetics and *Professional Budo*, the Greeks, the cornerstone of our Western civilization, far from being optimistic
rationalists as we are taught in school, were deeply pessimistic and believed the world a thoroughly irrational place
in which human beings were the playthings of the gods and
were constantly subject to pursuit by the Fates and Furies.

The Chinese, especially Confucians, also held this view.
While the world was an orderly place, it was nonetheless
completely subject to *Ming* or Fate.

Even to this day, primitive people perform intricate rituals to appease the gods and Fortune. And this doesn't only
happen in California. Every society has its own version of
cults and irrational social movements as anyone can find
from even the most cursory reading of Freud, Jung, or
Reich.

But, if such irrational practices are so widespread, are
they necessarily "wrong"? To answer that one I simply would
ask the reader to remember a time when fate played into his
or her life. The tire pops, the roof collapses, your kid is
arrested, the boss calls you in. There is no warning, nothing
you can do. You are alone. You are completely helpless.

Is life irrational? You bet.

When the corporation decides that your job and those of
a lot of middle-aged people just like you have to be sacrificed
to Mammon, all the vitamins, meditations, diet, and every
conceivable New Age tape are not going to be of a whole lot
of comfort to you. Perhaps sacrificing a chicken would make
you at least feel better.

If the world is so irrational, however, how can one live?
How does a person deal on a day-to-day basis with Fate?

In *Professional Budo*, I gave the Confucian answer: Act
virtuously no matter what is happening to you. Basically, this
is a "buy and hold" or "dollar cost averaging" philosophy. In
other words, if you keep acting the same way, at least part of
the time you'll be right and, by not worrying about how to
act, you'll be under less stress and generally feel better. Back

9

to the New Age tapes.

This is okay as far as it goes, and, quite frankly, moral strength will hold a person in good stead over the long run and that is its point. However, sometimes life and fate require a direct answer. Now we are approaching the subject matter I would like to handle.

In the *Hagakure* by the Samurai Jocho, it is said that when the samurai is in a situation in which life and death are just as likely, simply choose death. One can thereby be assured that while one may not be successful, one will not, at least, be dishonored.

Now that is just fine, but what if a person wants to be successful? To be successful means that one gives the right answer to Fate, or, the giant problem facing one.

This raises a problem that none of the self-help literature seems to answer: Is there only one right answer for any given problem? We'll examine this more in the second chapter, but for now let us unequivocally answer: Yes and no.

To defeat a problem one has to prevail or win. A person wins against fate not by having the teacher give you an "A," but by knocking the hell out of the problem and stepping over its bleeding corpse. This is no exaggeration but is, in fact, the basis of every hero-myth from Perseus and the Sea Monster, to the Minotaur, to St. George and the Dragon, to Indiana Jones and his various assailants. The hero triumphs over the monster and gains the treasure. Bingo. End of story until the next monster comes along.

What we are talking about here is killing monsters. The problems we are concerned with are those that back us into a corner and with fangs dripping and claws clenching start inching slowly and decisively towards us. Here reason is of no avail. A good diet only makes you a higher quality cut of meat. And monsters don't like New Age music.

This is the area where the irrational, out-of-nowhere, overwhelming problem facing you must be met, not by rational discussion and thought, but by the full bore of your own irrationality. In other words, it's time for you to get creative.

Most people don't think of themselves as creative. Time to throw this book in the can; Katchmer's not talking about me. Not so fast! When most people think of creativity, they see somebody plastered with clay in the sculpture studio, or slumped over a desk writing the great American novel. But creativity isn't as confined as most people think. As I demonstrated in *Professional Budo*, creation occurs any time a human being forces his or her freedom as a person onto the world, the given. It can happen to a plumber, a cop, an artist, a student, a farmer, anyone. Quite simply, whenever a person thinks of a new or different way to do something, they are being creative. Think of your own life. Wasn't there a time when you were up against it? Time was running out. You didn't have the right tools to do what you'd always done in this situation in the past, so you winged it. You made do. You made it up as you went along. And you said you weren't creative!

Again, think of that moment. The moment when you pulled it out of your ear. Were you proceeding rationally? Did reason, did your normal way of doing things have any-thing at all to do with what you did to meet that situation? The answer is, possibly, to a point, but basically no. So there it is. Everyone, and I mean everyone is not only capable of creativity, but has in fact, acted creatively in their lives. It is what it means to be a human being, rather than a car engine or a computer or a can opener. Human beings are all creative by virtue of their human nature.

The second thing we can glean from thinking about our moments of creativity is that they are intrinsically and unde-niably and utterly—irrational. There is no good reason why you acted like you did, but you did and it worked. You made the bully laugh. You used a paperclip instead of a cotter pin. But you didn't get beat up and the shower doesn't leak. You don't know how you did it, but there it is.

We are all creative and we are all irrational. And that's

not bad. That creative irrationality is our weapon when we are backed into that corner by the monster problem.

Where does this irrationality and creativity come from? A better question would be: Given a world such as ours, subject to fate, how is rationality itself possible?

There is, in reality, no such thing as "the world." We all, each and every human being, are our own "world." We carry it around with us like the shirt on our backs. You don't have to look any further than the newest self-help book on the best-seller list to realize that the premises of all self-help books, tapes, and philosophy is that we, in our minds, create the world we inhabit. It is trite but true that the "world" of a beautiful, intelligent, healthy, rich person is quite a different world than that of an ugly, sick, poverty-stricken person. To a certain extent, of course, we can change our "world" by changing our mental outlook. The ugly, sick, poor person can begin to take more time with his appearance. He may pay attention to what he eats. I don't mean, of course, that he will wear Estée Lauder perfume and suddenly start frequenting the Happy Carrot health food store, but within every person's control is the ability to be careful and concerned with his appearance. To be clean. To be a bit more positive. These simple things improve one's appearance to a certain extent. One can also choose to eat vegetables and fruits for the same price as junkfood. This would make one feel better and also improve one's appearance. So we can accept the fact that the world a person inhabits can more or less be affected by his or her mental outlook.

There is a solid, philosophical basis for this idea. From Kant to Sartre, Western thought has held that the world we inhabit is created according to the structures of that mental faucet filter—the human brain. The world does not dictate, the mind does. World and mind affect each other.

Given that there are, therefore, no clear boundaries to either the world or a person's mind, is there anything objective or real in any of this? Or is life just a subjective, irrational mess?

If we think about it, what we really mean by "objective" is that which has an existence independent of mine. It acts on its own and while I may be able to affect it, I cannot make it cease to exist by a simple act of will. In other words, I can't just change my mind and it will go away. To believe that such a thing is possible is to be in the realm of the usual self-help, pop psychology outlook exploding on the book and video shelves. The world, while we can affect it, is real and objective—just ask anyone who has been hit by a car or been subject to recurring nightmares.

If there were no such thing as an objective world beyond my mind, we would not be having this discussion and there would be no such thing as religion or psychology. The objective world, not our subjective minds, create the type of problems we are talking about, and it is best that we understand our enemy so that we can see its weaknesses clearly and can arm ourselves accordingly.

The real or objective wold has two parts; two humongous, infinite Oceans between which our egos bob like infinitesimal corks. The human ego is a bruise, a mosquito bite, where two pachyderms rub cheeks.

On one side of the ego is the "external" world. This is the realm of physics, chemistry, biology, economics, and history. It is the realm of skinned knees, bent fenders, and layoffs. This is what we generally think of when we think of "objective reality." However, there is another reality on the inner side of the ego, equally infinite, and equally beyond our control and, obeying a law and logic all its own. This is the world of what Carl Jung called the collective unconscious and just as no physicist can tell you where the material universe ends, so no one can also tell you where the inner universe ends.

The conscious human being is the gate between these two infinities. And this unique position is the spot where human creativity becomes possible.

Why do I say this? Because as the gatekeeper between worlds, every person has the ability to open the door at any time to let the creatures of one world mix with or do battle with those in the other. It is an awesome power.

Carl Jung has primarily been the thinker who has studied and documented this process. Indeed, his whole extensive, compulsively Swiss system of psychology boils down to this one principle: That both the external and the internal worlds in all of their infinite creation and variety, if mixed properly, would result in the grandest thing in nature—the healthy human being.

Jung's insights came from the study of medieval alchemy and magic. The alchemy Jung envisioned, however, was a blending of the functions of sensation, thinking, feeling, and intuition, along with all of their symbols in both the internal and external worlds, into the great mandala spoken of in all of the world's religions—the whole and integrated human personality.

This was also the goal of Chinese alchemy as shown in my book *The Tao of Bioenergetics* and the works of Dr. Yang, Jwing-Ming and Master Ni, Hua Ching.

If we accept the fact that we are, in reality, the connection between two infinite sources of power, we begin to see how it is possible for creativity to spontaneously occur, and that the power is there for all of us to overcome any problem facing us. We only have to open the gate or complete the connection. This should be easy for us. It is our nature.

A good many of us will reply to all I've just said, "Nice sermon, turn up the New Age music, but my life is so busy, so controlled, that I don't have either the time or the place to even begin to breathe, let alone be 'creative.' The report was due yesterday. The kids have soccer practice. The house needs cleaning. My ulcer is acting up. My life is too jammed up. There is just no room for any of this."

So now you're asking the "How?" question. Okay. You accept all of this stuff about being a gate between two oceans of power. But so what if there is no way to use it? My answer is that you just have to make it and it's not as hard as you think.

We come to the idea of "holes" which is the central concept of this chapter. If I can't convince you of anything else, let me convince you that you, among others, (like your kids) have the power to "poke holes" in your life, and it is in and through these holes that the creatures of the other world can seep in and be the glue for a new model.

I'm a Buddhist. Hooray for me. The ideas I am about to present, however, can be applied to any outlook, philosophy, or creed. They are basic to an analysis of human life and all forms of creativity.

Since we are talking about basics let's start with basics: Just what are we? A body, a mind, a soul? We can find any number of philosophies, religions, or belief systems that will answer this question by pointing to one of the above possibilities. And they are all wrong. We are none of these "things" and that basic fact is what makes everything possible.

Long ago Anglican Bishop George Berkeley demonstrated that what we consider material reality—a reality that includes our physical bodies—was, in fact, nothing more than a collection of perceptions: sights, sounds, textures, all of which undeniably have their terminus in the mind. Therefore, since the mind and the mind alone can generate any one of these sensations without a material object being present, there is no need to believe that any material objects exist.

The mind itself, as David Hume asserted, can be subjected to the same analysis. What do we know of a mind beyond the viewing of individual thoughts? Given that all we have is a chain of such thoughts, why do we need to believe that there is a "thing" called a "mind" beyond them which we can never view?

Finally, and I don't mean to offend anyone, the concept of a soul also fails to pass analytical muster. How can we tell that we have a "thing" called a soul? Are my perceptions of the physical world my soul? No, of course not. Well, then, are the random streams of individual thoughts that run through my mind my soul? No. Then why would we believe in or need an extra "thing" we cannot see and which serves no purpose? Does the soul hold everything together so that I can be a unique individual? If everything is a group of perceptions in which ideas of the external and internal worlds mix, such as a woman I might be attracted to, in which my perceptions of her physical beauty and my perceptions of my emotional longings mix to create my idea of this woman I love, then, there is no real boundary to my idea of this woman and if there were, my idea of her would then become just one more idea among others and structurally indistinguishable from them. A soul is simply not to be found in this free-floating stream of perceptions that is human life.

If I am not a body, a mind, or a soul, then what am I?

As I said, I'm a Buddhist. Buddhism gives its answer beginning with an analysis of the human being and the world.

The world and all its objects or "things" is simply a "heap" of *dharmas* and the gaps between them.* It is these gaps that make creation possible.

A *dharma* is a moment of perception. It is neither internal nor external. It just is. It is separated from other *dharmas* by the void. Nothingness. Since there is no perception of, or, in this gap, it is called an "unconditioned *dharma*." Now the nice thing about something that is "unconditioned" is that anything is possible with it. It is here, in this unconditioned space, where we can let creativity into our lives.

Someone will, of course, object that this is nonsense.

---

*I am aware that my use of the term *dharma* is not the one that usually comes to mind. The primary definition is "law or truth." It also means one's spiritual experience or life path. However, another accepted meaning of this word is "element of experience." That is the way I am using this term. I derived this usage from the highly challenging book *Shifting Worlds, Changing Minds: Where the Sciences and Buddhism Meet* by Jeremy W. Hawyard, New Science Library (Shambala: Boston, 1987), pp. 56-58. If I am playing fast and loose with this concept, which I believe is a legitimate use of the term, the fault is all mine, not Mr. Hayward's.

There are no gaps in reality. The world is a continual stream. It is solid. It is real. That all sounds fine, but let us, like the Buddhists, start from experience.

You go into your office in the morning, the Jensen file is on your desk. There's a summary judgment hearing on Tuesday, Old Man Jensen has an appointment at ten, you have to get his story together about the oil leases, and what about those Yankees! What a game, five hits in the bottom of the eighth, and Lisa, I just got to figure a way to see her again, I had fun last night, Fred would you get me a donut downstairs. I'll see you later, Jensen's coming in at ten. What is that crazy fool doing on top of that building?

Disconnected, disjointed, random. That is reality. It is composed of bumping, jostling streams of soft, fuzzy, particles called *dharmas*. Is there any connection between the Jensen file, in the example above, and the Yankees, and your date with Lisa, and the guy jumping off the other building? These events are like the plastic balls bumping into each other in the lottery barrel on television.

Since there is no connection between these moments of experience, the *dharmas*, there are gaps between them. These gaps are areas that are not enclosed, not defined by perception either physical, like with the eyes, ears, nose, touch, or, mental, such as thoughts, daydreams, dreams, memories. They exist and they are "unconditioned" in Buddhist terms.

What does "unconditioned" mean, however? If we accept that our lives are made up of a stream of disconnected moments of varying degrees of consciousness, then very much like a billiard table, the motion of one discrete ball of experience affects the motions of all the others. If I line up the balls to break, and assuming I am not the lousy pool player that I am in reality, I bang the cue ball smack into the center of the colored balls and start all fifteen of them flying to the bumper and back. As I run the balls, the motion of one affects the positions and motions of the others. The place on the table and movement of any ball across the felt is dependent, conditioned by the whole of the game; the movements of all of the other balls. This situation is called "dependent arising." This is the Buddhist model of human life, or indeed, the life of the universe and any particular part of it. Just like the billiard balls, my experience, my *dharma* at any one moment, is dependent, conditioned by all of the other movements in the universe from the dawn of time until the death of the present age.

But just as it would be impossible to play pool if the balls were all jammed together so that they couldn't move across the table, spaces, gaps are a necessary part of the game of life. But also like the balls on our pool table, whether a ball of *dharma* rolls through the spaces on the table or whether the space is empty, the space itself never changes no matter what happens in the game. Its nature and existence are neither determined or conditioned by the game and its frantic movements. Since these spaces do not belong to and are not affected by the game, I can do anything I want with them. I could fill them up. I could put in wooden pegs; I could lay in runners. These would alter the game and change its flow and direction. In short, since the spaces on the table are undetermined and unconditioned, I can do anything I want there. I can exercise my creativity in those spaces and alter the game any way I want.

As must be obvious, the gaps between *dharmas* are, like the open spaces on the pool table, a place where creativity can be let into our lives. They are "unconditioned," not predetermined so anything is possible in these gaps between the *dharmas* that make up our lives. The trick is to get into these gaps; to access them. How can this be done if we can't experience them either physically or mentally? There is a way, but we have to step back a second to see it.

Let us approach things another way. You may intuitively ask, "Okay, if there are such things as these gaps between my moments of experience, my sensations and mental processes, why can't I see them or experience them?" The answer is that this idea is not all that new to us. We experience it every time we go to the movies. A movie film is not a continuous movement of connected images, but a long series of still photos connected by blank pieces of film with sprocket holes punched through them. We don't see the sprocket holes or blank film because the speed of the projector blurs them into the preceding and succeeding still photos and gives the illusion of a continuous, solid, unbroken reality. If the film were slowed down, however, we would clearly see the gaps and sprocket holes in the film and the illusion would be broken. We might even be tempted to laugh at the artificial and unrealistic movement as the film got slower and slower and the pictures moved more and more in slow motion until they stopped entirely.

In life, the Buddhists call this illusion *Maya*. The image usually produced in the East is that of a spider's web. The web of *Maya* that catches us like a fly and entangles us so that we feel that we can't escape.

Now we arrive back at our question. How does one move into, use, or access these gaps in reality? How can we move in them and allow our creativity to fill them? By slowing down the film.

We in the West have heard so much nonsense about meditation over the last four decades. Cows won't give milk. Meditate! Betty Sue doesn't love you. Meditate! Can't find that part for your '72 Pinto? Meditate, you fool! There is an enormous amount of ignorance covered by this single word.

In spite of this, however, people who practice meditation do claim to have more vivid lives and to be better able, more creative, in dealing with life. How is this possible when our usual image of meditation is escape?

When most of us think of meditation, quite frankly, we see a person sitting cross-legged in a quiet space, completely removed from the real problems and hassles of the world. "Make time for yourself." "Do relaxation techniques."

"Learn not to take things so seriously," we are counseled. Meditation, however, is not and cannot be removed from life. How could it be?

If, following our analogy, life is very similar to a movie, then meditation is the process of slowing down the film. First, we gradually see reality for what it is, a string of discrete, still pictures, dependent for their illusion of movement upon all of the pictures coming before and after. The only real movement is caused by the jerking of the sprocket holes in the empty space between these discrete pictures by the movement of the electric projector. The holes, it is seen, are where the real action is.

Eventually, with intense practice, the film can be stopped. This is the intermission. *Samadhi.* The stopping of the movie. During this time, one can do what one wants. Smoke in the lobby, hit the john. Paint the Mona Lisa. This is free time, or rather, no-time. The film is stopped, after all. And, here, is the gate that we spoke of earlier.

In order for us to be truly creative, which is, as we've stated, an irrational process, we must open the gate and let the two worlds, the inner and outer infinities, seep into each other. This, of course, happens accidentally and unconsciously as Freud has amply demonstrated, but in meditation, we consciously create the circumstances for this to occur. The door is purposely opened.

In the East, meditation is done a number of ways, but the main division between techniques is those that are done without images and, those that are done with the aid of an image to get one started and to direct the meditation. Actually, the method that does not use images is the preferred method since it is more like the unconditioned state we are trying to enter. An image, physical or mental, is just another *dharma*, after all, among other *dharmas*. However, as the Buddhist texts point out, to cross a river, the river of *dharmas*, it is okay to use a boat. Let's take a sail just to see the other shore.

An exercise that I have seen in many other places would be a good starting point. Go somewhere quiet. No, I am not asking you to "escape." I'm asking you to have fun. This is not in any way serious, okay? Sit cross-legged on the floor. We might as well do this right. Be sure to put a pillow under the roll of your butt to tilt you forward a bit. It's just more comfortable that way. Close your eyes. Breathe. My nose is always stuffed, allergies, you know, so it's okay to breathe through your mouth. I don't care what Swami Hobbinagoodtime Vishnuwerehere says. It's okay. Breathe any way you can.

All the books say to concentrate on your breathing. C-O-N-C-E-N-T-R-A-T-E. Doesn't this ring of constipation? If you are squeezing this out, go sit on the toilet and stop wasting your time. This is fun, remember? Watch your breathing, but don't get anal about it. That's the other end, okay? The reason that we are watching our breathing is so that we can feel it naturally slow down.

Slow down!? But isn't that just what we want? Of course. And the body does it naturally. Now, when your breathing has slowed, and your body has relaxed—come on, let those shoulders droop—let your buttocks spread out on the pillow and—joy of joys—this is the one place where, male or female, you can let your belly sag. We give prizes for the saggiest belly here. Surprise, as a sagging bag of flesh—you're really relaxed. Good.

Now let's look at that evil little gremlin—your mind. Your body is sagging and happy as a pig in slop. Your breathing is slow and following its own natural rhythm, but your mind wants to party. Roll out the keg, crank up the music! Open the window! Get the neighbors! Rah! Rah! Rah! This guy is annoying. How to handle your hyperactive mind?

The first thing is to see your own thoughts for what they are: disconnected bits of stuff floating around in a void, kind of like dust motes in the sunlight by an open window. Watch them float around. As you watch them, strangely, just like

21

the dust motes, they get slower, more graceful. It's almost like a slow-motion light ballet. Now look at the dust motes, your thoughts, floating in the sunlight, but then look at the light itself, not the motes. The spaces between the motes of thought. As you look deeper into the spaces, you at first still see the motes dancing in the air, but gradually, you won't see them any more. Now you are where you want to be. Now we can really have fun.

Let's make something. This is like arts and crafts time. Or you can think of it like woodworking in your garage. Or model airplane building. Or tossing a pot. Nice images, right? Okay, let's make a door. It's all quiet. The door is made out of colored air. We spray it on the empty air in front of us with a multi-colored spray gun. A light, fine film. Any colors you want. We move from the bottom to the top. First the frame. Then we plunk in the hinges. Then the door itself. It is plain. The door itself is not important. It is functional. It is a door. It has a plain, glass handle. We stand back. It's a door. We made it. It works. Wow.

Now let's open this thing to make sure we did a good job. Take the handle, turn and smoothly pull the door open.

What do you see? Don't think. Don't criticize. Remember what you see. I don't care if it's Sister Mary Margaret on a velvet swing in garters eating pound cake. Remember it and don't criticize or tinker with it. Now smile, wave, and close the door.

We're coming back to the planet called Everyday Reality. It is easier and faster to do this than to get to where we just were, Oz. All you have to do to go back to "normal" consciousness is to want to. Just tap your heels, Dorothy.

Do me a favor. Write down what you saw. Use as much detail as you feel comfortable with. As you do this exercise, the details will come on their own. Again, don't be hyper or anal.

When you've finished, sit back. Look out the window. Pet the cat. Clear your head. Now, read what you wrote. Read it again. Try to see the image again. Okay, now what does it mean? Again, let the thoughts come. Write them down automatically. DON'T BE CRITICAL! Make sense? Does it say something to you about your life? If it does, or if it doesn't, do it again. Write down your thoughts on the thought you just had about the image you saw in meditation. Oh, by the way, you were meditating. Do it again. And again. Comment on comments until you feel that you're done.

A funny thing will happen. As the chain of comments progresses, it becomes more and more rational and meaningful. By golly! You understand what the other side had to say to you! It does talk! And you know how to translate!

Welcome to infinity.

Let's recap, shall we? You, little ol' you, have just slowed down the stream of *dharmas*. You, you meditation master, you, have just pierced the Veil of *Maya*. And you thought you had to speak Sanskrit and stand on your head! You have been in the gaps between *dharmas*, in the unconditioned *dharma* itself, and you have viewed another world—and brought something back. Not a bad way to kill a little time. And I only use that phrase half-facetiously. In short, you, yourself have seen that you can do it. You have done it. You've probably done it before, but nobody told you that you had done it. Now you know. You know at least one way to access the unconditioned *dharma*.

Having done that, let me ask you a question, Effendi. Does your boss look quite as intense to you now? Is the Jensen report really as heavy a weight on your shoulder as you thought? Guess what else you picked up in Unconditioned *Dharma* Land—the insight and feeling that you simply don't have to BE THERE.

I study karate. The basis of all karate, no matter what style, is the concept of *Mawai*—or distance. If you control the amount of distance between you and your opponent, he or she cannot hit you. Remember the film *The Karate Kid*? The smartest thing Mr. Miyagi said was that when the punch came, "don't be there." One of the 14K golden lessons of

23

meditation is that there are other places to be.

Another question. Do you know why the European nations established vast colonial empires and virtually conquered the globe in the nineteenth century? Huh? No, seriously. Do you know why? It was not that the Europeans were bigger. It was not, we can all testify, that they were smarter than the people they subjugated in Africa, Asia, and the Pacific. Nor was it even superior weapons, which certainly didn't hurt. It was the one thing Europeans do really well. The Europeans' secret weapon. Collective discipline. Of course, other peoples have discipline. Look to any Yogin, or, for that matter, to the early life of the Buddha and you will see rigorous self-discipline. But that is the point. It is self-discipline. Individual discipline. The Europeans do it as a group thing.

During the eighteenth century, the Turks were making one of their periodic attempts to break into Europe. On a field in Eastern Europe, the Sultan's army, fierce, mustachioed, strong, virile, brave men all, were shocked to see what the Westerners put in front of them. A small force of French soldiers faced the Sultan. They wore clean white uniforms and powdered wigs. They were clean-shaven and had no huge swords. Instead they daintily carried muskets and powder and shot in what looked a lot like a purse. The Sultan sneered and asked, "Who are these girls?"

Well, the "girls" tore the living hell out of the Sultan's grand army that day. The Turkish corpses laid heaped upon each other in the sun. Why? Because the French lined up in neat, overlapping rows. They never broke ranks. They fired in precise volleys and obeyed the orders of their officers to the letter. They were a modern, disciplined force.

As people who have been brought up in the heritage of Europe, no matter what our sex or race, we in the West are trained from childhood to handle every situation like those French soldiers who confronted the Sultan on that day so long ago. We line up. We face the enemy head on. Never break ranks. Fire in volleys. Always, always obey our officers. That my friend, is our genius and our downfall. (Lest we get too smug, let us not forget General Custer, General Gordon, and Dien Bien Phu. It doesn't always work.)

The point of all of this, besides showing that I read a lot of unconnected material, is that we, like these old soldiers, are taught from childhood to deal with our lives and, more damagingly, our problems in one rigid way. How often have we heard, "You can't run away from your problems," "You have to face up to things," "Meet it head-on." Well, if you and I were walking through the woods and I looked down the trial and saw a copperhead sunning himself smack in the middle of the path, and I told you, "Don't go there; there's a copperhead in the way," would you go down that path?

But this is precisely how we are trained from grade school on to handle our problems. Number one, who says you can't run away from your problems? If Arnold Schwartzenegger was mad at you and was pounding on your door, wouldn't it be a lot better to dive out the back window and run? Or maybe sneak up behind him with a two-by-four? Somehow these solutions sound better to me.

If you don't like the idea of "running away" from your problems, how about running around them? We see examples of macho men doing this several times a week. It's called football. How smart would it be for a halfback to get the handoff, scan the line, and then run smack into the opposing three-hundred-pound tackle? No, the entire game of football is based on "not being there." Offensive linemen have one purpose in life—to open holes in the defensive line so that the backs can skip through. What is a forward pass other than a method to put the ball where the other guy isn't?

Armies maneuver. Why? So as to out-flank or encircle the enemy. Why? To be where the other side isn't. Is this cowardly? Of course not. It is the key to all victories.

But we are told, "Stand up and face your problems head-on." Do you want to know who says this to you? Quite simply, someone who wants to control you or who could care less if you get hurt. If you move, you can't be controlled. That is why boxers bob and weave. Don't "be there," choose your ground.

I wish that I had a dollar for every employer I've ever had who went to sleep at night comforted by the thought that I couldn't leave and find another job or another way to make a living. One of the most depressing of these situations was when I worked as a loan collection officer for a major East Coast university.

I worked with about a dozen other people, all of us in our mid-twenties, in a small, poorly ventilated, underground room. The vault was there and so were the old freeze-dried foods from the Cold War. "Duck and cover" signs could still be faintly made out on the cinder block walls. In the summer there was no air conditioning and your sweat dropped and stained the loan forms. To be a manager in this section of the University, you had to be condemned by a tribunal at Nuremberg. This was during the recession in the mid-seventies and I had just graduated from college with a degree in philosophy. I was lucky to be working anywhere!

I lived sumptuously in what I can only describe as a torpedo tube. It was actually an oversized closet on the second floor rear of a brownstone. The toilet was down the hall and I knew the roaches by their Christian names.

My employer in the person of his manager, Eva Braun, never tired of reminding all of us that we were greatly privileged to be licking her boots, and no, there would be no raises.

I endured this for three years. One day I decided that I had to be able to do something else. There were no jobs since there was a recession but something had to give. But what could a humble philosopher do? Well, philosophy students argue. They read. They research. They write. They argue some more. They make personal attacks on their colleagues. It hit me! I had the skills to be a lawyer! Lawyers get paid to argue. Lawyers get paid to do research. Lawyers get paid to make personal, scurrilous attacks on their fellow human beings. And they get paid well! That settled it. I would go to law school.

So I became a lawyer. But you know what? These people at my old job had really ticked me off. Now since the one advantage of working for a university is its liberal vacation policy, I decided to take the seven weeks of vacation I had built up and get out of the office while they paid me. I wouldn't be there. I went to Europe.

When I returned I had a month before school started. I can't say my heart was in my work. A certain lightness had taken hold of me. My boss seemed, somehow, uh, less substantial in my life. I won.

The point is that I could very well have sat around moaning about only being a philosophy major with no discernable skills. Many of my loan clients defaulting on their student loans, people much better educated than me, were doing that very thing. Sometimes the cobra hypnotizes you. Remember, you don't have to look it in the eye.

My best friend at this job also was dissatisfied. His story was more bizarre than mine, however. First, he just plain quit—after having his doctor write a note stating that his ulcer was a result of stress from the job. We were computerizing. He got unemployment.

Next, he moved out of university housing and down to a more bohemian section of town. He spent the next six months reading and living off of his vacation pay and unemployment. One day he announced that he wanted to go into film production. That was interesting since he had even fewer skills than me. But he had visited that place where things can happen.

Through friends he got the names of a couple who produced TV commercials. He hand-delivered his resume, such as it was, and parked on their doorstep. He groveled. He sacrificed small animals. He made vague promises about doing anything. They finally hired him as a gopher just so he'd stop bugging them. Within a year, my friend was in charge of purchasing and was an assistant producer. It was totally insane—and it worked.

By the way, this same guy eventually had a falling out with the producer. Again he was unemployed. This time he blew his savings on computer equipment and training, and has spent the last five years freelancing as an editor and graphics designer and has done quite well, thank you.

Don't ever feel that you have to face down the cobra. It's far better to use your head and not "be there."

A final note on the cobra thing. What happens when you have a John Wayne-style Western fixation with staring down a cobra? All of your energy is absorbed by the cobra. Soon you are drained and you are unable to get away and save yourself. The cobra poisons you and swallows you. You become a big bump in the cobra's belly.

I'm not being facetious about this. What do you think depression is? It is the withdrawal of usable bio-energy from your system. This can happen in a number of ways. First, you can just simply give it to the forces opposing you. You can feed the cobra on your own energy. Maybe if you stay till nine instead of seven every night, the boss will notice. Maybe if I make his breakfast "just so," he won't hit me. Maybe if I increase her allowance and give her a car, my kid will love me. You're feeding the cobra and when you don't have any more to give, the cobra will eat you.

A second way we waste bio-energy is to absorb it into our own mind and muscles. When we unproductively soak up all of our energy in our minds, we call it a psychological "complex." Examples are obsessions and compulsions, even masochism. When we tense up so much that the living energy can't flow, it is called "armoring." The rigid, tense musculature serves exactly the same function as steel armor to a knight. It is a shell that protects the person from external blows. The only problem is that you can't feel anything.

You're dead and you just don't know it. Also, you can't move. And there you are stuck in front of the cobra again.

Life, a healthy life, which necessarily includes self-respect, requires the free flow of biological energy within you. As Chinese medicine also teaches, this energy radiates out from you when you are healthy and well-balanced. This energy is yours. It was given to you at birth, according to Chinese thought, by your parents and by the Universe. You have every right to use and enjoy it. Nobody and nothing has the right to restrict it or steal it from you.

Accordingly, the first step in dealing with any problem is to deprive it of energy. Withdraw your energy from it, don't feed it. If you withdraw your energy, it becomes smaller and you become that much bigger. You can then act from strength and freedom.

My friend and I, from the above examples, could very well have stayed in the same job. We could have put our energies into hating the boss, hating the university, and worrying about our inescapable fate every night. Freedom came when we said "enough." When we started to put our energies elsewhere. Let me personally tell you that just the simple act of changing the flow of your energy is an exhilarating experience and by doing so, you start to feel alive again and your self-awareness and self-respect start to grow.

Again, a short exercise. Sit down. Feet flat on the floor. Get comfortable. Close your eyes. Don't get quite as comfortable as you were when you were meditating. Okay. Envision your energy. Think of it as a cloud or a liquid. Now gather it into a ball around you. Feel it flow from the ball into your veins and arteries, your lungs, your nerves. It goes through your whole body. It is cool and clear and refreshing. Like a breeze. Now think of something really distasteful that you had to do today. Don't let your energy go to it. You are in control. Keep the thought at arm's length. It's over. You're just looking at it. You, not it, are in control. That feels better already. Now examine this thing like it was a bug on a pin. Turn it over. Look at it through a magnifying glass. Odd, isn't it? A curious specimen. Take one more good look. Yuck. Throw it away. You have the power to do it. Still have all of your energy? You should, you're in control. If you feel like you've lost something, pick it up again. Look at it even closer. It can't bite. It's on your pin. You're in control. When you realize that, throw the damn thing away. Much better. How do you feel?

You've looked at this thing and you've managed to keep your energy intact. Look to tomorrow. Pick another distasteful thing that you have to do. It, too, is a bug on your pin. This one is still wiggling, however. It's not dead yet. But it's your pin and you're in control. Keep your energy to yourself. It's yours and it feels good flowing in you. Why would you want to give it to this "thing"? Yuck.

You know what? It isn't getting your energy. It's slowing down. Good. Watch it. It's stopped moving. You didn't feed it because you didn't want to give up your energy and it died. Examine it again. Curious, isn't it? Oh well, now you can throw it away.

Breathe and with each slower breath, feel the cool flow of the energy through your body and around you. It feels like a slow, cool wind upon your face. Enjoy it until it slows and stops. You absorb it and feel good. You own your energy and you don't have to give it away or hide it in your mind or in your muscles.

You know, of course, what you can do with the energy you've saved, don't you? You can take it with you and channel it into the unconditioned space, the gap between the dharmas of your life, a place that you know how to get to at any time you want.

Why would you want to take this energy with you into the unconditioned space in your life? Because the gate between your worlds is there. You can use it to achieve things on either side of your door. Everything needs energy and sometimes the things you are seeking from that part of yourself behind the psychic door in your mind must be attracted and fed. The important, and I mean important, thing to remember is you are in charge of the feeding process. You can cut it off anytime that you please. In the material world, if you stop feeding a stray cat, for instance, it goes away. The same with the very real and just as independent beings and things in the world of the psyche. If you invite something in and it misbehaves, starve it.

That, however, should not be a problem because you are offering only positive, clean energy since you have withdrawn it from all the things that would contaminate or pervert it. You are always in charge.

One final look at the uncontrolled *dharma* that you have entered. Think of this space as your workshop. The energy that you bring is like the electricity that a person uses to run their power tools or appliances. The materials you need are either in the external, material world, or, behind the door of your psyche. You can make anything you want in this undetermined, uncontrolled, free space. This is where we begin to solve those unsolvable problems.

It's an illusion to think of life as a seamless web in which we are trapped like flies waiting to be eaten by a spider. We have all poked our fingers through spider webs. In reality, they are thin and flimsy. We make our holes so that we can have space through which the infinite creativity that we all have within us, just by virtue of being human beings, can flow. In this space we can make anything of our lives because here we are what we really are as human beings—existentially free.

If there is nothing else that I have convinced you of in this chapter, let it be that you, like Don Diego, are much more than you seem. You are, in fact, the doorway between two infinities. In that position, as a human being, you have the enormous power of a gatekeeper. As a gatekeeper you also have the power to determine where your energy will flow. With this power and your ability to direct it, you can solve and overcome anything that has become an obstacle to you. You are Zorro. If you believe this, we can go on. If not, forget it. Put this book back on your shelf or wrap it up and give it to someone you don't like for Christmas.

CHAPTER TWO | **Making Problems for Yourself**

I live in Dayton, Ohio. It's boring. I work, as I've stated, at least for the moment, as a prosecuting attorney. Despite what you've seen on TV and in the movies, it is also boring. One of the high points of my existence in Dayton is to occasionally go to lunch with an old friend. Somebody shoot me, please.

One of my longest standing friendships is with a guy named Mike. Mike is from a New York Italian family and is, naturally, a shy and retiring individual who never loses his temper. He is also generous to a fault and exceedingly funny when he gets hyper about something, which is, of course, infrequent, given his Italian heritage. He is also one of the best and most dedicated trial attorneys I have ever met. Then again, I live in Dayton.

Mike is a family man and lives with his wife and two daughters and a Siamese cat about two blocks away from my family in a huge, upscale house in the better half of the upper-middle class community where we both live. We're both lawyers with working wives, after all.

Our particular plot butts up against what used to be an old, crossroads town in west central Ohio. The boonies, by any other name. Recently, however, it has been "discovered"

33

by developers and professionals like myself and Mike. So those Reaganesque housing developments sporting houses that would use the Taj Mahal as an outbuilding, but with no lot to speak of, have surrounded the huts of the yeoman who formerly held sway in this shire. The yeomen don't like it.

When our town was a Norman Rockwell memorial, sports reigned supreme. Rough, inbred, set pecking order, no-outsiders-need-apply, rural versions of football, basketball, baseball, and soccer. Unfortunately for these good fellows, the outsiders have now applied in droves.

The yeomen, however, still control the Youth Athletic Commission. It is an hereditary aristocracy, as all aristocracies are. These kind folks control who gets on what team. In short, the teams for youth sports are stacked. Nowhere is this more apparent than in Little League baseball. Both boys and girls.

Mike's oldest daughter is athletic. She loves all sports and is good at them. This last year, she decided to play baseball and Mike being the doting and middle-class brainwashed father that he is, agreed to coach. He soon discovered he wasn't in Kansas anymore, Toto.

It came as quite a surprise to Mike, an innocent in the Byzantine intrigues of the local Youth Athletic Commission, that one of the teams in the league happened to have about a half dozen of the best girls thereabouts. The other teams, including Mike's, were, uh, not so good. Quelle Surprise. Mike didn't like this, but he was a sport and a highly competitive trial attorney so he managed the girls with the same intensity that he managed his trial docket.

Mike, the brash interloper, practiced and practiced with his girls. Strangely enough, they won their first game. Then they won again. They weren't the most talented team, but they were well-coached and they had heart. They next met the Russian Ladies Baseball Team, aforementioned, and were soundly trounced. Nonetheless, Mike's girls won enough of their games to be tied for first place with the

Russian Ladies.

The baseball season in our sleepy hamlet extends well into July. There's not much else to do. At any rate, many people, especially those from the developments, start going on vacation at this time. Mike suddenly found that three of his best girls were leaving. It was at that time that the evil baseball commissioner decided upon a playoff for Number One. Mike wanted to set the date for sometime before the players left. The Commission stalled. The coach of the Russian team was seen chewing tobacco at the general store with the league commissioner. They set the date for after the girls left. Mike, rationally, more rationally than Mike is wont to do when being cheated, suggested a tie for number one and trophies for all. Mike even offered to pay for the trophies. Nothing doing. The game was set for a week from Friday. Mike was down three good players and except for his daughter, who was usually his catcher, and one of his pitchers, he was down to the scrubs.

What was Mike to do? The problem was how to play without his three best players. Or was it? Mike, who was coached by the same football coach as me, Black Ron, we called him, below decks, didn't see the problem that way. Mike, as all winning coaches do, framed the problem another way: "This is what I have, now how do I win?"

Mike didn't focus on what he didn't have, the three girls, but on what he knew that he did have—a decent pitcher, and, at that level of play, a decent pitcher was a very handy asset indeed. Mike knew that this girl could pitch fast. Nobody had encouraged her to do this because accuracy in the Little League is more important than speed. The time was now past for such genteel considerations, however. Mike started teaching this little girl to throw smokers. Her father took a week off from work to practice with her. By Friday night, she was hurling thunderbolts.

The teams met. The pitcher left the Russians swinging. By the fifth inning of this six-inning game, Mike's team was ahead four to nothing. Then, under league rules, he had to change pitchers. The other team immediately scored five runs. In the top of the last inning, with the other team's scrub pitcher also in, Mike's team scored two runs. They were again leading by six to five.

Unfortunately, the other team's batting order was the top of their lineup. All of the stacking was about to pay off. The first girl got up and hit a long, long ball to center field. Mike knew it was all over. Nobody, however, told the little girl, the scrub of the scrubs, playing centerfield because at the last second she put up her glove, and, look what I found, the ball dropped into it. One out. Mike was elated. He made vows to light candles and print mass cards. But he knew in his heart it couldn't last.

The next bruiser came up. She hit a clean drive to left field. It was downhill from here, Mike knew. The third girl in the order, a killer, was up. Mike told the pitcher to walk her. Two girls on. First and second. Now it was the clean-up batter at the plate. First pitch, a burner between first and second. Mike's daughter, who usually was the catcher, had to play first in this game because the regular first baseman was gone. She misjudged the ball and it whizzed right by her. The runners took off. Again, however, nobody told the little girl playing second that she wasn't any good and therefore should not be able to stop a line drive. This girl managed to knock the ball down. She quickly tossed it to the shortstop who was a regular and got the out at second. The other runner, was being waved to home from second base by the overconfident friend of the evil commissioner who was coaching third. He had not seen the play at second. The tying run was heading for third.

Meanwhile, the shortstop burned the ball to home to cut off the run. The girl who was now catching for Mike had never been a catcher before. She was totally out of her depth. Mike was already thinking that even when the inevitable happened, it had still been a good game.

But the inevitable didn't happen. The girl at home caught the ball and went into the most professional catcher's crouch this side of Yogi Berra, completely blocking the plate. By this time, the errant third base coach had seen what was happening and as his runner rounded third, HE GRABBED HER and pulled her back to the bag. League rules state clearly that a runner may not be touched by a coach or it is an automatic out. It was a double play! Mike, when he was revived, found that his girls had won the league championship in spite of all the odds!

The commissioner had the humiliating honor of having to award the trophies, on the spot, to Mike's team. Mike was gracious. He thanked his girls, and then he thanked the commissioner for allowing his team the chance to play for the championship—after his three best girls had gone on vacation. Then he gave the commissioner a free Italian lesson. He taught him the meaning of the word *vendetta*.

Admittedly, there was a good deal of luck in this story about this girls' Little League team. But there is also an important point buried in it. The power to frame a question includes the power to answer it. As stated, Mike could have said to himself, "What can I do now that I'm missing my best players?" That, however, would be a pessimistic way to frame the question, and the answer would necessarily be negative. Instead, Mike asked himself, "This is what I've got, now how do I win?" The difference, of course, is that the second question assumed that he could win. That's quite a difference. Every problem that we face in life involves the asking of questions. When confronted with something that needs to be resolved, typical questions are, "How did this happen?" Or, "Why is this happening to me?" Or, "What did I do so this is happening to me?" And finally, "How do I get out of this?" Or, "What do I do now?"

Sometimes we don't recognize what's happening to us. We ask questions such as, "What is this?" Or, "What does he or she mean by that?" And, "What does this mean?"

These questions come automatically and are of no help whatsoever. They show ignorance and imply helplessness. All of the power in the situation is given thoughtlessly to the obstacle.

Have you ever wondered why we automatically react this way to a problem? Is it natural for human beings to just abjectly grovel in front of any opposition in their lives? I suggest that it is not, or as a species we'd have never left the trees in the prehistoric forests of our ancestry and some other species would be coaching Little League games, growing beards, and hunting human beings in December at Human Camp in the mountains surrounded by cases of beer or whatever creatures from that species use to cloud their minds at sporting events.

The human species is a species of accelerated innovators and survivors. That is why we are masters—and I am not a humans-first kind of guy—but the facts can't be contradicted—we are masters of the planet and are dribbling out slowly into the solar system.

If it is not natural for us to act like deer in the headlights when faced with adversity, then this attitude must have had to have been taught to us. The question is who would want to teach such a life-negative thing to the majority of the human race? Well, to whose advantage would it be to have a large pool of sniveling and helpless creatures? Those who want to control us, of course. Those who want to lead and to tell everybody else what to do. This includes all of the petty despots of all of human history: All of the bosses, lords of the manor, dictators, landlords, abusive spouses, high priests, generals, and know-it-all relatives with whom one comes in contact. My father used to call these people "Little Napoleons." They are the petty office tyrants and control freaks we all encounter in our normal everyday lives. If you don't need them to make your decisions for you, they lose all control over you, and, like the bug on the pin in the last chapter, they soon stop wiggling and die for lack of power.

A woman I know worked for years for a social agency helping the disabled. She was a counsellor and a good one. She loved people and she lived to help. She is the most compassionate person I have ever known.

Sometime during the mid-eighties, during the general conservative drive to reduce paperwork in government, all social service agencies suddenly found the number of their governmental forms quadrupling. The corresponding forms for the local polluter meanwhile were reduced to a postcard from the beach, but that's another story. This woman's agency, due to the pro-management bias of the times—this was, after all, post-PATCO—decided they needed a new, tougher management style and they needed to weed out the older employees whose salaries, due to decades of dedicated service to the disadvantaged, had exceeded what the new order was willing to pay.

So they contacted the West German prosecutor's office and the Mossad and obtained their lists of war criminals. After scouring their resumes, they finally found a woman, blonde, spiked-heeled, complete with riding crop and monocle, who fit the bill, and put her in charge of everything.

Her first step was to hire a hatchet-person. (Note the politically correct rendering of this noxious fact.) Her hatchet-person, oh, let's call her Ludmilla, was a scrawny, prematurely graying product of the parochial school system.

Ludmilla had a plan. She was a clever one, she was. Her plan, which by the way, coincided nicely with that of top management, was to bully, browbeat, and harass the older, competent staff out of their long-held jobs. This, of course, would lower the labor costs for the agency. This was important because the superintendent had just purchased genuine Louis XV furniture for his office and needed to reduce direct care staff to pay for it. Meanwhile, money became so tight for some unknown reason that staff had to purchase their own pencils since the agency couldn't afford them.

Ludmilla's next step was to replace the veteran, and lest

we forget, competent staff with her former employees from another division. These people all had had disciplinary problems, that is, incompetence, emotional problems, and some, substance abuse problems. They all had the virtue in Ludmilla's eyes, therefore, of being totally and abjectly dependent upon her. She had been the only thing that stood between them and their just desserts—being fired. They also had the virtue of being willing to spy on their fellow employees and report anything and everything that went on in the agency. This is how control freaks work. And Ludmilla was in control. She remained in control for eight years and then left to head her own agency. It is, in short, the Ludmillas, the Little Napoleons of the world, who want more than anything for us to automatically freeze and feel helpless in the face of any adversity or challenge. It keeps us in our place and under control.

Unfortunately, most of us have received so much of this training in fear and helplessness from our childhood on that we have internalized it and can be helpless all by ourselves now. We don't even need a Ludmilla anymore. But, as pointed out in the last chapter, such an attitude is counterproductive and steals your energy—which you must have in order to be at all creative in your life.

So, once again we need to take control. We need to take our energy back. Before you do this, however, you have to kill your boss.

Before doing this delightful little bit of wish-fulfillment, however, let me make two preliminary points.

First, DON'T LITERALLY KILL YOUR BOSS! This exercise is to be fun and help you feel better. A protracted trial, intense media attention, commercial endorsements and book deals are not all that they are cracked up to be. Please don't actually kill your boss. I'm a Buddhist, and I don't even squash mosquitos, so let the bugger live.

Second, so that I won't be misunderstood, I am not anti-management. I am pro-individual. You may very well be the first vice-president and chief operating officer of your company; responsible for the total day-to-day operations of a firm that does business on five continents in seventy-five different currencies. But—your boss is the president and chief executive officer and you know what he does. He plays golf, he goes to his club, he breeds horses, and the hardest thing that skunk does is to look at his wing-tips and tell you that your work is not quite up to snuff and by the way, the board is considering downsizing. He must die. Top management such as yourself are people too.

Now, let's go to a quiet, comfortable place. A place that just naturally makes you feel really warm and good. Take off your shoes. In fact, get naked if you feel like it. This is your show, your ritual. If you want to paint your face or wear a horned headdress, go right ahead. The feeling you want is one of power.

You must sit up for this exercise. Your spine should be straight. Your muscles, however, as with all of our exercises, must be relaxed. Do the breathing and relaxation procedure that we did in the last chapter. Go through the thought flurries like in the last chapter, and again arrive at your open place. We don't want a door yet, however. Right now, we are going to do some painting.

Next to your feet you will find a bucket and a wide brush. The bucket is full to the brim with bright, searing red paint. Take the brush and get some paint—it doesn't matter if it spills—and slap it all over the walls. Throw it around until the whole space is covered in hot red paint. Breathe very deeply. Absorb the red color into your system. Breathe into your toes. Breathe the whole way down into your genitals and finally into that place at the bottom of your being, what the Chinese call the *Huiyin* cavity, the spot on your perineum halfway between your genitals and your anus. Let the red energy flow out and spike into the earth, grounding and balancing you. Feel your hidden power mix with the volcanic power, the heat of the magma and lava hidden in the earth.

Let this molten power spread though all of the channels of
your body. Your veins and arteries, nerves, lungs, nasal cavity, eyes, ears, and acupuncture lines of force. As the energy
builds, let it push out from your body into a hot, radiating
field.

Now, pull all of this energy, as much as you can get, back
into yourself. Feel yourself stuffed to bursting with hot energy. Allow your normal color to return, feel all of the red
around you seep into your body through the cavities the
Chinese say are in the soles of your feet.

You look normal. You look like yourself. Nobody would
suspect the red power that you have hidden within you. Now
it's time to make another door. An office door. You look at it
calmly. You muse about it. You know what you will do.
Nobody else does. This gives you great power.

Knock on the door. Your boss opens it. (The boss can be
a he or a she, of course, but for the sake of clarity, let's say
the boss is a "he.") He has his usual sneering, condescending
look on his face. You, however, smile pleasantly. You have
the power. You walk in.

Your boss starts his usual routine. You know the words,
so hear them just as they are always spoken to you. He now
wants you to give an explanation. Instead, it's time to tell
him off.

Tell him anything and everything you want. Don't be
analytical, don't limit yourself—say anything that comes to
your mind. Get obnoxious, swear, anything you want to say.
The important thing is to say it all.

He is shocked. He may try to come back at you. If he
does, repeat this process, say everything again. Do this again
and again until he finally shuts up.

You are finally in control. It's time now to let the power
that you have hidden within you out. Your skin starts to glow
and vibrate, your color is turning pinker, dark pink, red,
electric red. Waves of red energy are emanating from your
skin. A quarter of an inch, an inch, three inches, a foot.

Extend your field as far as you like. Your boss is startled. Eventually, the field touches your boss and zap! A charge flies from your solar plexus and slams him against the wall. He is pinned and then falls to the floor dead. The power crackles in his body. Look at him. Enjoy this moment. You are happy. There is no pressure in you anymore. You are relaxed. The tension has been discharged. There is one thing left to do. That energy crackling through the corpse is yours. You need to take it back. He has no right to it. Open the hole in your solar plexus. Allow yourself to suck your energy back in. Imagine that there is a giant pot or cauldron there open to receive the energy.

As the energy returns you will see that it is a muddy, ashen, sooty black and gray color. You don't want to keep it that way. It is poison. You must now hold it for a moment and purify it. You don't want to discard it because it's still usable energy and it is yours. Put the lid on the cauldron. Let the full pot descend into your abdomen. The Daoists have a practice called "fusion" in which different energies, even negative emotional energies, are mixed and purified and then this increased energy is spread out again through the body and mind and used. Emotional energy, even negative emotional energy, is very, very powerful. As you hold the energy in you, do not let it leak. It is in the cauldron or pot which you have allowed to descend into your abdomen. Heat the pot. Feel it growing hot. Hear it bubbling. You now need to attach a tube to the pot to the air outside of you. Allow the light, blue energy from the heavens into your pot to mix with your captured energy. The darkness is lightening up. It is becoming a rich purple.

Another tube is necessary, one from the earth. It runs through the cavity in your perineum and up into the pot. Solid, thick, rich, golden earth energy pumps into the mixture. There is now a gently rolling, creamy, sweet energy in your caldron. A third tube, a valve, lets the pure silver steam escape from the sweet liquor. It goes around through a series of cooling coils and distills into a cool mist. This mist escapes into your heart and is pumped with your blood, your *Xue*, in Chinese medical terminology, to every corner of your body. It enters the nerves and you feel good. Really good and at peace. Breathe and enjoy this. You are free. Enjoy it until you want to go back to Kansas again.

I'm not telling you that you are suddenly free from all your problems. After all, we didn't really kill your boss. But again, we took power from him or her. Now you don't have to rely on him or her as a source of power—and answers—for yourself. You know that you have the power to be the source to tackle your own problems.

So here we are again. The obstacle remains. Now, however, we are free to approach it. Like in *The Wizard of Oz*, we have earned the right to make demands of it. To ask it our own questions. The ones we really want answered and in the way we want them answered.

Since I've got you in a receptive frame of mind, let's talk a little bit about questions themselves. Most of us are scared to death by questions. Questions imply ambiguity. They imply that things are not as they should be. If you have to ask a question, then you don't have the answer. You don't know something. Most of us usually feel that if you have to ask somebody something, then you don't have the power and they do. That's the reason we killed your boss, so that there is no longer a person with power over you. You are the source.

To think in these terms about the nature of asking questions is to make a terrible mistake. Instead of losing power when you ask a question, you are actually asserting your own power. In effect, you are saying "no" with every question you ask. When you say, for instance, "Is this chair four feet high?" you are raising the possibility that it is not four feet high. If not, if you knew that it was indeed four feet high, why would you ask the question?

An even more interesting type of question is the "really"

question. Now either something is something or it is not. Is this really a chair? It raises the possibility that this object is not a chair. It secretes negativity into the world. The "really" question, in addition to injecting negativity into things—a basic property of all questions—also invokes a whole system of metaphysics, specifically Platonism. To ask if an object is "really" a chair implies that there is some standard by which we can tell what a real chair is. Where does this "real" chair exist? Why, in the transcendent forms of all objects existing in the mind of God. Get it?

Questions then, are not as simple as we like to think and perhaps it's the fear of the void, the fear of nothingness, which is raised by questions, that makes us so nervous about asking them. When we ask a question, we come face to face with the possibility of our own nothingness.

We've learned, however, in our study of the unconditioned *dharma*, that the void is a friendly, open place. It is the place where everything is possible, just like the space created by a question. A question is, in fact, a magic spell, words of power, that pokes a hole into our lives, once again tearing the web of *Maya* or illusion.

Why do you think that no dictator welcomes questions? It is simply because a question implies that every illusion, every pronouncement of the dictator and his entire propaganda apparatus about the way things are could be just plain wrong.

Jean-Paul Sartre, the French existentialist philosopher, said that it was the nature of man to question. By questioning, the human being was in fact, saying "no" to things as they are. The human being is a doubting being and by raising questions and saying "no" to things as they are, the human being asserts his or her essence which is—freedom.

For those of us who have raised children there was that wonderful time when they learned how to use the word "no." They learned that they could say "no" to their parents. This was maddening for the parents, of course, but as parents we all knew that this was a necessary stage in the child's development; a first step in the child's developing an independent sense of self. In other words, the child is asserting his or her power and freedom as a human being with each little snotty, maddening "no."

The same principle runs throughout human life. If we do not ask questions we are not human. Back to Toddler 101 for a refresher course.

It is a mistake, then, to fear to ask questions. Instead, the real fear should be with those who are asked a question. It is they who must make something real. And they are at a disadvantage from the outset since that metaphysical "no" is always hanging out there.

Again, we get our fear of asking questions from our upbringing. Authority figures are in business to keep power for themselves. Therefore, they feel on a visceral level that to be subjected to questions is to be picked dry of their power. Better to train people not to ask questions.

We see this problem everywhere. Recently, my son had a question concerning his math homework. My wife and I, being social service types, were naturally no help to him whatsoever. He was in a quandary. He didn't want to ask any of his friends because he thought he would look stupid. In other words, he thought that they would have power over him. He was afraid to ask his teacher. The teacher had apparently done his job quite well. After about an hour of being totally frustrated, I remembered something that happened to me when I was going for my MBA.

One of the required courses was economics. This was not Economics for Idiots, but the real thing with real mathematics and formulas, etc. I worked for hours and hours on my homework. I read the examples. I worked the problems. I yelled at my wife and kicked the cat. And I still did lousy on the quizzes. I was afraid to approach the professor, but I couldn't understand how everybody else in the class was doing so well. So I asked my first question. I asked a friend how they could understand this stuff. She told me her method and that of everyone else in the class. They all went to the professor on his Monday afternoon office hours and he gave them the answers. I had been incredibly stupid!

I told this story to my son, who loved to hear me call myself stupid, and in appreciation for making his day, called a friend and got the answer.

You must ask questions. It's okay and you gain power from it. If you can accept now that it's okay to ask questions, let's do a two-step exercise to see how it feels and specifically to feel the power coming to us from asking questions.

The first exercise is the simplest of the two, although it might seem like the toughest. I want you to pick any situation during your week, the one where you feel the most intimidated, the most powerless, and I want you to pick a person from that situation; a person who you believe has power in it. It doesn't have to be the person with the ultimate power, but it must be someone with some power. Wait until you are actually in that situation again and ask that person a question. Any question. Ask them if they think it will rain. Ask them if they like your tie or your hair or for directions. It may be a superficial question, but it has to be a real question. No "How are you?" kind of stuff.

My brother works in the wine industry in California. He has over the years trained my family how to savor fine wines. I know it looks pretentious and asinine in movies and TV, but you really can savor a fine wine. It coats your tongue, it activates different taste buds in your mouth. It is subtle, it is rich, it is complicated, and it is warm and immensely satisfying. How did you feel after asking a question and getting it answered? Forget the answer, that's the least important thing right now. How did it feel to ask and to control? Taste the power. It is only a little sip, but even a drop of a fine Cabernet is enough to enliven the whole mouth. Note everything, every nuance and flavor of your sip of power. Get to know how power feels and tastes.

Do all of this again. When you feel comfortable with it, ask follow-up questions. Let your mind go. Do it until you feel satisfied. Make yourself do it until you feel thoroughly satisfied. You'll know when that is because once again, you'll feel relaxed and balanced. You won't be able to think of anything else to do or ask. It's almost as good as sex. Well, it's fun, anyhow.

One other thing about this exercise. Pay attention to the responses of the person of whom you are asking questions. Note their reactions. They must perform. They are under pressure. If you have had any doubts as to where the power lies in a question relationship, their responses should clear that up for you.

The second part of this exercise on questioning is designed to enhance the feeling of power that questioning gives. A note on power itself: It is always felt. It is always associated with the feeling function. It isn't an intellectual thing; it doesn't come from the senses. It can enhance sensations and quicken the mind, but those are only results, not the power itself. We need to really get the feeling of the power of questions.

The reason that I said that the first part of this exercise was the easiest was because you did it in the external world with real people. There really is only so far you can go with that. People clam up. There are interruptions. You don't have the privacy to totally enjoy yourself.

In this exercise, we are once again going into the uncontrolled *dharma*. We don't have to be as rigid as we were when we killed your boss; we can relax a bit more. Take any position in which you are comfortable. Make your way into the *dharma* space like you have before. You don't have to be naked, or in war paint, or wound-up this time. In fact, I want you to just be yourself. Wear something that is really you. If it's jeans and a sweatshirt, fine. If it's your flannel nightgown, fine again. Just something that you really feel like yourself in.

When you are again in the unconditioned space, we need

to travel back in time. Is this possible? Of course. This is the place of infinite possibilities. We are going back to a time at the very beginnings of civilization. It is a time that is still half-wild and only barely civilized. Objects are made of bronze and copper; there isn't any iron or steel yet. Now you have to construct a rustic sea coast. The trees, pine trees, run the whole way down the slope to the edge of the water. It is night. The water is gray like the color of the full moon overhead. Granite cliffs jut out from the tree line. A cold, damp wind comes off the water and pushes us up the hill. We are here on purpose. We are going to see the Oracle.

The Oracle is a person who sees into both worlds. We know nothing about the Oracle but this and that it lives in a cave above the tree line. I say "it" because no one really knows the sex of the Oracle. Sometimes it is male, sometimes it is female. More than likely it is both sexes. It draws energy from two sets of genitals. Because of this, it is impossible to tell its age. It sometimes appears as an old, old man, and at others, like a pre-pubescent girl. It wears animal skins and leans on a roughly carved wooden staff. A clay food bowl sits at its feet. You are going to meet the Oracle. It is expecting you. You will ask it questions, and because you ask, you honor it and make it happy. Because you ask it questions, it will answer.

Do you feel afraid? Why should you? You already know that the Oracle wants to answer you. It wants to transfer its power to you.

We approach the cave. It is dark inside. Now, call your Oracle. Call it by any name you wish; Fred, Ethel, Ozzie, Harriet, David, Ricky, or Spot, or, make up a name. It really doesn't matter. What matters is that you are exerting your power by calling to it.

Out of the shadows, emerges the Oracle. Wait until it is completely in the moonlight. What does it look like? Make a note of its appearance. How do you feel now that you are face to face with it? Note your feelings. These are your feel-

49

ings when you exert your power. If you are uncomfortable, watch your breath, let it calm you down. Wait until you are comfortable, then sit down. Your Oracle will sit across from you. Look deeply into its face. What do you see? Make a note of this also.

Now begin asking questions. Anything that pops into your head from whether you should kiss on the first date to the meaning of life. The content doesn't matter. Only the feeling of asking a question matters. But remember your questions. Listen for the answer. Pay close attention to it. Remember the answer. All of it. No matter how nonsensical, remember it all. Ask another question. Watch the Oracle. Does it change its appearance? Remember its changes and what question you asked when it changed. Remember the answer.

Repeat this process over and over again. The Oracle doesn't mind. You are only flattering it and making it happy by asking it questions. It wants to answer. Ask and ask again until you feel there is no more to ask. You don't have to thank the Oracle. You have done it a favor, but say something nice to it and bid it to leave in peace.

Before it has time to slip away, write everything down. The questions, the answers, the changing appearance of the Oracle. Be sure to do it in sequence, just as you did it when you were there. Put your writing away.

Wait two days. When you have some quiet time, and can concentrate, take out your record and read it. Read it again. Does anything strike you? Why? Write down what and why. Does anything mean something to you? Note what and why. After you are satisfied with your notations, write a short commentary on what you've learned from them. What you think the message is. During the next few days, occasionally think of your message. Go back, make notes again. Write a new commentary. Do this as often as you feel you want to. When you are satisfied with it, put it aside. How do you feel? Hopefully, you feel much stronger, more centered. A power unto yourself.

At this point, we need to stop for a second and clearly see where we are. These exercises are designed to allow you to withdraw power from wasted places in your life. They are designed to help you learn to generate your own power. Power is a wonderful thing and it feels damn good! But while the savoring of your power, like the savoring of a fine wine, is a joy in itself, it rots if it is not used in the real world. Make no mistake, the power is itself real. There is no illusion to this. Everyone from the Chinese *Qigong* masters and alchemists, to the Western depth psychologists such as Freud, Jung, and Wilhelm Reich will attest to its reality. You are welcome to study the science of this in my book *The Tao of Bioenergetics*, or in Dr. Yang, Jwing-Ming's book, *The Root of Chinese Chi Kung*. But it is much more beneficial to actually use the power you have generated. After all, this power is inexhaustible and using it, as all sources agree, only increases it.

I don't want you to become so introverted that you lose touch with that other infinity, the external world. We use the internal world, after all, to enhance and extend our external world. That is the point.

While asking questions gives one a sense of power, this power, like any other source of power, can be either dissipated and wasted or just plain dangerous if it is simply generated and let loose to flow in any direction. You will generate energy by doing the exercises I have outlined so far. This energy can do a number of things. It can make you hyper and scattered, or, it can activate materials from the personal unconscious which you might just as soon let alone. Or, you could feel super for a few days, as the energy leaks away, and then crash into a terrible depression. Energy must be properly channeled. You must know what you want to do with the energy you've generated.

At the end of World War I, the victorious allies, the Big Four, Britain, France, the United States, and Italy met at

Versailles to basically carve up the map of the world and dictate peace terms to Germany. Since most of the war was fought on French soil, the French had a huge incentive to create terms that would forever remove the threat of a strong and armed Germany. The French also were no slouches at the game of diplomacy, having invented much of it. Therefore, when the world leaders, Wilson, Lloyd George, Clemenceau, and Vittorio Orlando from Italy met, the other three allies were in for a big surprise. While the Americans, British, and Italians expected to discuss and negotiate the terms of the German surrender, the French plopped a written agenda onto the table. Since the French controlled the agenda, all subsequent questions had to fit into that agenda and all answers came from the conclusions that the French had already incorporated. All roads led to Paris, so to speak. The French very neatly channeled all of the energy of the Allied victory towards the ends that they wished to accomplish in Europe. The Germans had to disband their army, pay a crushing war indemnity, and, when they couldn't pay, the French occupied the mineral-rich Saar region, using colonial troops from Africa, who scared the daylights out of the blonde-haired Germans who had never seen black people before. Of course, the German right wing had its own agenda, which was deftly channeled into the agenda of an ambitious ex-soldier named Adolf Hitler. Channeled energy is enormously powerful.

The failure to properly channel questions and the energy they raise is as destructive as the proper channeling is productive.

Due to the problems with the economy and the anti-taxation movement of the eighties and nineties, many school districts in Ohio faced for the first time the failure of their tax levies. Classes, teachers, extracurricular activities, and even bus service were all cut in response.

My own local district was one of the best in the state. People moved into this district specifically for the school system. As I've said before, what was once a rural area had attracted large numbers of professionals and their families. Professionals view education as the key to success. Schools are, accordingly, high priority. Levies always passed.

A few years ago, I was contacted by the school system and invited to a meeting ostensibly concerning how to improve the school system in the future. When I arrived, I found that I was one of a group of about fifty parents, all obviously professionals, upper middle-class, and all obviously school boosters. The good feeling quickly evaporated, however, when it became obvious that this entire meeting, instead of being a free exchange of constructive ideas, was actually a set-up by the superintendent and an outside consultant that was intended solely to rubber-stamp a plan to completely rearrange the classroom facilities, purchase a school-wide computer system, and build a new junior high.

None of these ideas were bad in themselves, but as the meeting progressed, it was obvious that the deal had already been cut and there was really to be no alteration in Das Plan.

This being America, things got nasty. In other words, the questions began and the Super was no Clemenceau. While no one had a problem with more computers—in fact such an idea was very appealing—did the school have a lesson plan? Some idea of how they would be used in the curriculum? Uh-uh. Okay, then how did they know how many they would need if they didn't know how they would use them? Uhhh. Since the space requirements for these new computers would require extensive renovations of the existing buildings, how could we approve such renovations if we didn't know how many computers would be needed? The Super was getting angry but trying to hide it. After all, we were his biggest supporters in the district. If we balked, he was dead.

Then there was the question of cost. There were, of course, lawyers and accountants in this crowd. Well, the school administrators didn't know what they needed specifically, but this was how much they were going to ask for in the new levy they would present in the next general election. Oh, and by the way, the reason we were all there was to give our support to and work for the next levy.

It was not a good evening for the superintendent and far from getting a rubber-stamp approval, nothing was resolved. Another meeting was called. It was scheduled for eight on a Saturday morning in February so that most of this nasty crowd wouldn't show up. I did anyway.

At this meeting, parents responded that they might support building a second middle school if the lower grades, fifth and sixth, would go to one of the two middle schools, and, the upper grades, seventh and eighth, would go to the other. The way things were presently, all four grades were mixed in the two existing schools. The parents, rightfully or wrongfully, felt that the older kids were just a bit too mature for the younger ones. But implicit in their response was the positive message that support for Das Plan would be forthcoming if this concession was made.

The superintendent rose to the occasion. He snatched defeat from the smiling jaws of victory. Separating the grades was not, for some reason, a part of Das Plan. The Super then feigned his inability to understand the parents' abundantly clear request. He began asking questions, inane questions about the parents' motives for wanting this change. The parents would answer and he would repeat the answer, only it was not their answer, it was his answer the way he wanted to hear. An example:

Parent: I am afraid of having older kids mixed in with my fifth grader. He's just too young for them. They're almost in high school.

Super: I hear you saying (Social Service Speak) that if you weren't afraid that there were older kids in the school, you would support Das Plan? Right?

Parent: Well, uh, well, if I weren't afraid. I guess so.

Super: (Triumphantly) So you would support Das Plan?

Parent: Well, uh, I, uh, guess so.

Super: Good. Now, here's the plan for the new middle school.

After the meeting, I spoke with some parents and teachers in the hall. At first everyone was bewildered. What had happened? Then everyone got real, real mad. It was so obvious to them what had been pulled in there, and, worse still, the negative energies generated by their originally good intentions, that were subsequently squelched, were left unresolved, hanging out there. Now all of this energy turned to resentment. Welcome to Germany between the wars.

This was an enormous blunder on the part of the school hierarchy. It was a clumsy and obvious attempt at control without resolution or rechanneling. The Superintendent had deftly alienated the very people upon whom he had always been able to count in the pursuit of his levies. Needless to say, the levy did not pass and has not passed to this day. It was an opportunity to improve a superior school system and it was blown by the failure to ask or direct questions and energy correctly.

We have spent time in this chapter in getting used to asking questions. Any question. We've gotten accustomed to the feeling of the energy generated and the feeling of the power that comes from questioning. We have seen examples of the dangers and the rewards of channeling or failing to properly channel this energy. What do I mean by "properly channeling energy"? I mean to use our energy to successfully achieve any goal you have in mind—without wasting any of the energy you have generated. To do this, we have to know how to frame a question.

To understand how to ask questions we need to understand that there is never just one and only one way to ask any question. The thing to remember is that the way you ask a question to a large degree determines what kind of response you will get.

"You want vanilla, don't you?" Or, "Vanilla is okay, right?" is quite different from, "You wouldn't want vanilla, would you?"

Each question is about vanilla, but the first two almost force vanilla on the person questioned. The last question invites a rejection. Add body language and the first two questions are almost intimidating and the last is so negative that the person questioned would want to reject not only the flavor vanilla, but the person asking the question! A simple question concerning the flavor of ice cream, if improperly framed, leads to a personal rejection! We need to get this right.

In order to free ourselves from the idea that there is only one way to ask a question in any given situation, we need to practice the differing ways to frame the same question. To practice this, we are going to a carnival.

I'm old enough to remember when there were carnivals regularly making the circuit from small town to small town. All carnivals had a midway. That's where we're going. Let me take you there.

The one I remember best was just a small, second-rate thing that arrived in my home town, a dingy river town on the Juniata River, back in the hills of north central Pennsylvania. This was flannel cap and deer-hunting country. Another America entirely.

The carnival set up in a field at the edge of town, right under a pine-covered mountain. The lights were white and yellow bulbs on strings and the rides flashed with reds and greens. Some flickered because the bulbs were burning out. There was the noise of the calliopes, shouting, and bells. The smells of food, popcorn, hotdogs—which by the way are at their best only if boiled in kettles out-of-doors in the fall—and cotton candy.

We walk into the carnival. The lights surround us, but above, the mountain is dark and the pines make a jagged edge against the sky. There is no pollution here so the stars are white and the size of softballs.

We pass down the midway. Past the freak shows, past the

games. At last we come to the end of the row. It is a simple machine, standing by itself. The noise is muffled here and the only light is the bottom lighting of this particular game. An October wind, cold but clear, slips across our cheeks. This machine is a box containing the torso of an Eastern Swami, complete with a turban with a crescent moon on it. It's an old machine. Not electric. Just creaky and mechanical. All pig iron gears and handles worn by no-one-knows-how-many years of use.

There is a slot for pennies. That's right, it only costs a penny. The hundredth part of a dollah! One copper penny, kid! Step right up!

What you do is to put a penny in the slot, think of a question, and with both hands pull the big lever on the side. This is a fortune-telling machine. It will answer all of your questions.

Think of a question, any question about anything, close your eyes, grab the lever and pull with all of your might. You can hear the gears inside clanking and grinding and whirring. They echo into the chilly night and against the hills. The whirring goes on for a long moment. Let out your breath. You can see the steam. A colored paper ticket pops out of a slot in the Swami's mouth. What color is it?

Take the ticket, turn it over, your answer is on the ticket. What does it say? Remember your question and your answer.

We have all night. It's Friday. No school tomorrow. You have a pocketful of pennies. Ask it the same question, but in a different way. You want to know something more or different about your subject. Ask the same question in a different way. Put in the penny. Think of your slightly different question, pull the lever. The gears clank and grind. The sound is happy and relaxing. This evening is fun. It's a good time. The ticket pops out. It is a different color. What color is it?

Take the ticket. Turn it over. What does it say? It is not the same answer because the question was not quite the same. Remember the slightly different question and the new

57

answer. Repeat this process asking the same question in many different ways until you run out of pennies. Then leave the carnival and go home to Kansas.

You guessed it, I want you to write down all of the different forms of the questions you asked and all of the different answers. Also, if you remember, I want you to write down the color of the ticket that went with each answer. Now put these notes away for a week. Forget about them.

At the end of a week, get a cup of tea or coffee or juice or soda pop, and read over your questions and answers. First, notice how many different ways you were able to ask the same question. You can control how a question is asked. Next, see how the answers changed. Go through your list of answers. Is there one answer to this basic question that you like best? If so, look at how you framed the question to get this particular, satisfying answer. This is the question you should have asked.

Finally, check the color of the ticket on which the answer was written. This represents the feeling tone of this question and response. What does this color mean to you? How does it feel?

I want you to do this exercise a few more times. I want you to practice until you get the feeling of a good, direct question. Compare the ticket colors of the best questions and answers. Are they always the same? If not, what is the difference? Is it the subject matter? Is it your mental attitude when asked? If there is discomfort, try to visualize the most comforting color, or the color you want as the gears move. Keep this tone when you are exerting your energy by asking questions. It is a source of power for you.

Knowing that a question can be posed a number of ways and, knowing how it feels to pose a question in a powerful way, the next step is to ask the question in such a way as to gain the end you wish to accomplish. To win.

To do this, you have to know what answer you want. You are not asking questions in the context of power in order to gain information. That may occur but it is an added benefit. What you really want is to control the situation. To master your obstacle, your problem. You are directing energy at the problem. You want to crack it like a rock, not to leave it intact and simply be left with a wonderful, full-color portrait of it still sitting smack in your way.

The German philosopher Martin Heidegger said in the introduction to his groundbreaking book, *Being and Time*, that to ask a question means that you already know what type of answer you want. You already know at the moment of questioning what the answer should look like. There is, of course, a right way and a wrong way to get the answer you want. An illustration of the wrong way was provided courtesy of my local school superintendent. The Oracle exercise, however, should be a good guide toward asking questions in a way that feels right. You've learned how to ask a certain question. How it feels. You've also learned in your exercises in asking questions in general, in reality, and in posing questions to the Oracle how the person questioned reacts and how that feels to you. Now you need to combine all of this.

When Johnny Carson had "The Tonight Show," he used to do a character named Carnak the Magnificent. Carson would come out in a cape and a huge turban and be the mystic seer from the East. The premise of the routine was that Carnak would give an answer to a question before knowing the question. It's your turn to be Carnak.

I'm not going to go through all of the preparatory rigmarole that we've used throughout this book—but you should. When you're ready, *domine, domine, domine,* you are Carnak the Magnificent.

Think of an answer you would like to get, or a fact that you want to be true. Now, just like Carnak, or like the game show "Jeopardy" for that matter, make up a question to which this "answer" would fit. You know what's coming next. Make up another question for the same answer. Do this again and again. If you want some fun, put on some sitar music or something similarly exotic. You can be as zany and flamboyant as you want. As time goes on in this exercise, it should become eminently clear to you that this is all a joke. Not what I'm telling you, but reality itself. The joke is that the answers are always and already there. It isn't that you don't know the right answers, but rather that you don't know the right question. The questions are like the pennies you slipped into the slot on the fortune-telling machine. Put in a penny, pull the lever and the gears automatically pop out one and only one ticket.

It's like my friend Mike at the beginning of this chapter, "This is what I have, now how do I win?" It wasn't a mystery. He had obviously observed his pitcher all season. He obviously already knew she could pitch fireballs. The answer was to let his pitcher go to it.

We've seen in this chapter that the person who frames a question has the power over any obstacle if the question is framed in such a way as to direct the energy of a situation in a way that the inquisitor wishes to hear it. It is actually a magical act since it alters the reality of the situation and puts the inquisitor in control. The primary areas of control are the energy and feeling tones of the confrontation. Questions are not really verbal or linguistic matters, they are matters of power and in fact, invoke a whole system of metaphysics. The person who asks a question the correct way is in charge.

What then of situations where the answer is not readily apparent? Or more accurately, and more consistently with the preceding discussion, what of situations in which we, the questioner, the person faced with the problem or obstacle, doesn't know what he or she wants? This can occur either when the object or situation sends out confused or conflicting energies, or the person confronted doesn't know how he or she feels about what is being confronted. There are two possibilities in such a strait, either make an end-run and simply avoid the problem—"don't be there"—or, probe, explore, attempt to make sense of the problem for yourself.

I say to make sense of the problem for yourself because no problem is objective. They may have objective aspects, but all problems are problems for someone. That means that all problems, like the questions used to confront them, are intrinsically and basically subjective. In other words, the attempt to make your problems "objective" or the object of totally rational analysis is self-delusion, and mistaken. Mr. Spock is a fictional character. All problems are problems of feelings. There is no such thing as a purely intellectual problem.

When Bertrand Russell was working out the mathematics for his great book, the *Principia Mathematica*, do you think that when he became stuck on an axiom of mathematical proof, that he sat back calmly with his pipe and reasoned until the computer in his mind clicked out the proper and mechanical answer? Or, do you suspect that Russell stormed around his den, threw his pen, behaved abdominally to his wife and/or mistress and was a real shit until he found the answer that satisfied him? I've read his autobiography. I'll lay money on the second guess.

In the next chapter we will deal with methods for approaching enigmas, that is, problems towards which we are confused or ambivalent. We will develop methods there to make these problems more controllable and targets for the use of our energies.

CHAPTER THREE | # Making Sense of
the Senseless

In the last year of law school everyone's concerns and worries are not centered on the class work or grades. If you survive the first year, you have a very good chance of becoming a lawyer. In fact, in New York, where I was living prior to going to law school, if you told a woman you wanted to date that you had been accepted into law school, the stock reply was, "Talk to me after your first year." Law school was serious. In other words, you had a real chance of flunking out.

After the first year they knew that they had you and could begin to torture you in earnest. You survived the first year. You could take it. This was going to be fun. The second year they worked you to death. It was not unusual for me to brief 150 pages per class per night during my second year. In addition, I clerked for a municipal court judge and taught his class on constitutional law—for which I prepared approximately 150 pages per night—at the local community college. He collected the professor's fee; I collected my clerk's fees—a chicken, some cabbage, and a pound of flour per week. I was riding high. By God! I'd name my first kid after him!

At any rate, the third year of law school was the scariest.

This was the year in which you had to find a job.

We heard terrifying stats. Only twenty-five percent of students had a job offer by the end of the first semester, third year. Only half by the end of the year. I was lucky, I had an offer in New York—which I didn't take because my wife was pregnant and we didn't want to live in the city on what I was making at the entry level. But the offer did warm my cockles.

One of my closest friends who received not only a law degree, but an MBA, was hired by a transportation company. I obviously cannot give specific details since that would be a breach of trust. However, suffice it to say that my friend had no idea what he was walking into when he signed their black book.

The older management of this firm had all been executed. White hair, three-piece suits, and pools of blood. The same old thing. A group of young Turks headed by a balding, diminutive Grand Turk in his early forties had captured the company. Nothing was certain. Everything and everybody got a turn on the block.

Besides doing in the old men who had made the company, something had to be done about the company's fuel costs. Fuel was the largest portion of the company's expenses. It ran into the hundreds of millions of dollars and came from a number of suppliers. The firm was in the process of consolidating its routes and compressing its schedules. The new CEO, as with many in the mid-eighties, saw his way to stardom through cutting costs to raise the bottom line and also the stock price. Of course, no new sales, products or services were offered since that would have actually been productive and would not have fit in with the plans of the CEO who was already being measured for his golden parachute. The south of France or the Grand Caymans are nice this time of year, aren't they?

No, the new management would raise productivity the new-fangled way—by squeezing the rock to get blood.

Laying off long-time employees, cutting benefits, selling off painstakingly acquired assets and breaking the union—that was their strategy. For this, these visionary heros—in a further effort to help the bottom line—increased top management's salaries and benefits three times in three years, eventually quadrupling their beginning renumeration.

But back to fuel, the life-blood of the company. After helping in a few random executions and bouts of union-busting, just to make sure he was one of the club, my friend was visited by the vice president and general counsel of the firm.

The conversation went something like this:

Vice President: Uh, Frank (the CEO), uh, wants you, uh, to, uh, look at the, uh, fuel contracts, uh. Just see what's there, uh, maybe see what you can do.

It may not seem like it, but these were marching orders. Failure in whatever it was that the vice president was babbling about would mean instant death.

My friend, new and afraid to question the Emperor, read a dozen fuel supply contracts and their accompanying documents. He color-coded them at 5 a.m. in the law department's conference room. He wrote a report, complete with an executive summary and crib sheet with diagrams. It was presented to Frank, the Emperor of the Tiber, as he presided over the renegotiation of the employees' health care package while sacrificing sixteen-hundred Visigoth prisoners to propitiate the gods. Frank frowned. The document was returned. My friend was in disfavor.

Conversation:

Friend: Well, what does Frank want?

Vice President: Just look at the contracts and see what can be done.

Friend: About what? What does Frank want me to do?

Vice President: I can't tell you that. Figure it out. This is all bullshit anyhow. Just figure it out.

With this clarification my friend went back to the fuel contract. He dug into the company's financial records and discovered what it paid for fuel per year. He worked formulas—which he had to learn from scratch—and projected the amounts of fuel the company would actually need until the end of the contract period of the longest contract. He found that the company would be oversupplied with fuel and calculated the oversupply and the cost. He wrote yet another report, with graphs, and sent it to Frank.

Frank was meeting with private security forces which he intended to use after his next good faith bargaining session with the union failed, as he knew it would, and he was faced with keeping those uncouth pickets from exercising their First Amendment rights on the public roadways near company property. To seal the deal, he sacrificed thirteen-hundred Thracian slaves to Baal. He read the report and frowned again.

My friend and his wife and children faced disgrace and being sold into slavery in the market in Byzantium.

Conversation:

Friend: What does Frank want me to do!!? Does he want me to rewrite our entire fuel policy for the next ten years?

Vice President: I'm really disappointed in you. So's Frank. Maybe you need some help.

Friend: No! No! That, uh, won't be necessary. I can do it.

Vice President: Frank's counting on you, Centurion.

Friend: Hail Caesar.

Vice President: Hail Caesar.

My friend did, in fact, rewrite the company's fuel policy for the next decade. As a reward, he was visited by the firm's treasurer and number two man, who, flanked by two security guards, removed all my friend's papers from his office—just to keep them safe, you understand—and he was fired the following week, saving the firm yet another salary. Of course, they used every bit of my friend's new fuel policy, saving the firm tens of millions, helping management add new benefits to their compensation packages, and, buying Frank the CEO a new get-away vacation property, a castle on Cap Ferat on the Riviera, which he christened by immolating twenty-one hundred Scythians in games that lasted four days during the Saturnalia.

This, my friend, is what real problems in the real world look like. They are abstract expressionist globs. Free-floating sculptures that don't give the slightest clue as to what they are about—but which all have very sharp edges which will slice you to ribbons at the slightest wrong move. It is like being Captain Kirk or Captain Picard or whoever the hell is in charge of the Enterprise these days, and being dropped onto some God-awful planet where the carrots are purple and look like cabbages and there is this gigantic metal something following you and randomly frying your landing party with bolts of some unknown energy. Scottie's asleep and the transporter is broken. Good luck. It's like talking with my teenage son (supply your own form of misery here): Breakfast—at 11:30 a.m., Stardate 2940.2.

Me: Good morning, son.
Him: Aaaa.
Me: Why son, what is the matter?
Him: Aaaah
Me: Do you want to talk about it?
Him: You don't care!
Me: Of course, I do. Please, what's the matter?
Him: You didn't care two months ago on Michaelmas at 2 a.m. How could you care now?
Me: (Trying to remember Michaelmas at 2 a.m.) But son, I always care. Is it your school work?
Him: No!
Me: Your friends?
Him: Arg.
Me: Is it a girl?
Him: Dad! That's none of your business.
Me: There is a girl? (Shock)

Him: Dad!

Me: Is it bigger than a bread box?

Him: You make a joke out of everything! You see! You *are* filth and scum, and beneath my hormonal contempt!

Me: Son, please. What's wrong?

Him: Things.

Enlightened? I sure am. But he has a point. Sometimes, we are lucky if there is actually something objective to deal with. The roof leaks. Your division's sales are off. You can face these things. As we've seen, however, no problem is purely objective. There is always a mixture of the subjective with every problem and sometimes the problems are purely subjective.

This isn't to say that they are not real or that they are not serious. In fact, the more subjective a problem is, the harder it is to handle. With the more subjective problems, you have to add a huge dose of anxiety to the mix. You know something is wrong, but you're not sure what. You feel like you're missing something and that keeps you off balance. You keep running things through your mind but get nowhere. Because you can't define the problem, you aren't sure what the answer could possibly be or even if there is an answer. If you do something to solve the problem, you can't be sure that you are right. So you again run them continually through your mind. The resultant lack of sleep will really help you maintain a rational outlook!

Another species of the unsolvable problem is the Booby Trap type. These problems are constructed of equally bad alternatives. If you do "A," a horrible solution, then "B" will occur, which is totally unpalatable. You could do "C," but it is even worse than "A" or "B." Doing nothing will allow "D" which will destroy you. If you put the drug-dealing pimp on the stand as an eyewitness to the shooting, it will come out that your victim was at that location to buy drugs and child pornography. The jury could say "good riddance" and acquit the shooter. On the other hand, if you don't put on this sterling citizen as a witness, you have only a weak circumstantial case and the shooter may also walk. You could do a plea bargain, but you would be dealing from weakness and the wiley public defender would know that and ask that the murder charge be dropped to jaywalking with a firearm spec. Make a decision, Big Boy.

In both of these species of unsolvable problems, the Nebulous and the Booby Trap, the first thing to do, and the thing that will at least permit sleep with the help of sedatives, is to define the problem. Now, a clear definition of something that by definition is indefinable is not really possible. So the problem has to be trapped first.

There are a number of ways to approach the ungraspable problem. My personal favorite is to hack it up. Go at it with a meat cleaver. Some people will think I'm talking here about analysis. I'm not. I'm referring to butchery.

Take your undefinable problem as just that, as an indescribably disgusting and shapeless mound of entrails and guts. Yuck and double yuck. Okay. You are the master of the situation. You have the meat cleaver. Even in the most amorphous mass of stuff, there are things that stick out. Things that catch your attention. Argh! Start by lopping these things off. It doesn't matter if you're cutting at a joint or whether this is a rational break or an anatomically correct place to cut. Cut anyhow.

What I'm telling you to do is to look at the situation confronting you. You probably can't see it all and should assume that you can't. Pick something you can understand or at least some part of your problem that attracts your attention. It doesn't matter if it is a logical place to begin. Start tugging at the intestines and you'll find your way into the abdomen. The guts of the thing.

Ask yourself, "Why does this particular aspect of the thing stick out for me? Why is it so important to me? What is it connected to? If I pull this, what happens? If I push that, what pops out? Does any of this make any sense to me?" If it does, go on. Follow that lead. Remember, if you reach a dead-end, you can always hack off another piece.

As I've said earlier, problem solving, at least attempting to solve these types of problems, the Nebulous or the Bobby Trap, is not a rational procedure. Analysis would probably just get you killed. At the very least, it would be a waste of time. With the Nebulous problem, it would be like trying to catch a gas in a net and with the Booby Trap, you would simply end up where you started, recognizing that the problem confronting you was a mass of contradictions and bad alternatives—in short, a Booby Trap.

In the story about my friend at the beginning of the chapter, I don't want anyone to think that the vice-president who was tossing these undefined problems at my friend was stupid or a poor communicator. The reality is that most of the time people don't know what they want. Perhaps this is simply a reflection of our existential state of being as human beings. Whatever, we have all felt that we wanted something or were unsatisfied, but didn't know what or why. Given, therefore, that the person or persons wanting you to solve their problem don't themselves have a clue as to what they want, you suddenly have an enormous amount of power through your ability to frame the question, as we've seen earlier, but also an enormous amount of risks in that you also have to convince them that your answer is what they wanted in fact. Facing such a situation, doing something, anything, is just as likely to be correct as doing any other thing. Therefore, butchery becomes a fine art. Like the old Roman Augurs, you are reading the entrails. Somehow, this all pleased Caesar, and it has the advantage of giving you at least something to say.

I'm not being as facetious here as you might think. If you can accept the fact that a rational analysis of a problem such as this, that is, the Nebulous one or the Booby Trap, won't work, then some other function of your mind has to be employed. Either feeling or intuition or both. These are the irrational functions of the mind as laid out by Carl Jung and must be used when the rational functions, thinking or sensation, fail. The irrational, however, is not nonsense. Rather it has its own way of approaching things.

Remember my friend the attorney? None of the conversations with the corporate vice-president gave my friend a clue as to what was expected. Go back and read them. Nonetheless, my friend intuited what was really wanted, a rewriting of the corporate fuel policy. Unfortunately, it took my friend too long to let his irrational functions go and to act on them. He was fired not for the content of his eventual report, but for his failure to read Frank the CEO's mind! I'd ask you if you've ever been there, but I know you have. The point is that my friend's intuition was right. Had he recognized the fact that this was not a rational request, he could have kept his reason from getting in the way and getting him fired.

The same is true with my son, the adolescent boy. He was not communicating something that was coldly rational. Remember back to when you were an adolescent and your hormones were pumping? How rational were you? This doesn't mean that adolescents are stupid or bad people. What they are communicating makes a great deal of sense given their situation. They are submerged in hormones and they are communicating how they feel. Not what they think. Rational questions are of no help whatsoever and only provide targets for excess emotions. That's not bad in itself and will probably make the adolescent feel better, but most of us adults can't take such an emotional onslaught accompanied by all of the nice things our children say about us at such times. What is required is an emotional and intuitive empathy—not some sort of rational advice.

So what do you do, you ask, if you are basically Mr. Spock and don't have any intuition? Number one, everybody does. And number two, if you've gotten this far in this book and have done any of the exercises, you've let your mind crack open a bit and have already seen your intuition at work. Now just let it alone and it will take care of you.

How do the irrational functions work? They work in patterns and combinations. The patterns are constructed aesthetically, that is, for their artistic appeal rather than for their logical connections. Logic and rational thought only report on what is; the irrational functions, especially intuition, look at a situation and tell us what's possible. It is possibilities rather than logic that make us humans rather than machines. It is possibilities that make us masters of machines. Computers and, indeed, any other machine, are incapable of behaving irrationally. Irrationality in a machine means death. In a human being, irrationality can mean that too, when one has become more and more narrow and rigid in one's repertoire of behavior. But more often it means that one has become freer to be creative. Creation is the joining of human freedom with what is. Freedom transforms what is given into art. Art and creativity allow for possibilities. They transcend or overflow what simply is.

Going back to our attorney in the transportation company. His failure was not a failure to get the right answer. His failure was in not feeling the possibilities that Frank's vague request offered. He failed to match his intuition with Frank's. Was Frank an inarticulate boob? If so, how could such a nimnul rise to be CEO of a major corporation while still in his early forties? No, Frank intuited that something was wrong in the fuel supply system. He was searching for validation and some creativity from my friend. Unfortunately, my friend was a lawyer and, well, enough said. Frank's intuition offered my friend an opportunity which my friend's rational mind failed to recognize and respond to, or rather, and I hate myself for saying this, resonate to. In such a situation the "answer" is not a part of the data, but is made from the data and the free creative mind.

Back to entrail reading. We've stated that the irrational functions like to work with aesthetically pleasing (to them) patterns. Okay, let's take your problem. As you recall, we used a meat cleaver to reduce your problem to a mass of disconnected entrails slopped on a metal table. We've also had you identify parts and pieces that caught your attention. Now you have some familiarity with this mess. So what do you want to do with it? Look at it. Is there any way it's arranging itself for you, in your mind?

Start to see it that way. Help it. Draw it out or physically arrange it that way. Does one set of pieces suggest further arrangements? Arrange them. Keep going until you have a picture that you like. Remember, you don't have to use all of the parts. Some are aesthetically irrelevant. Put them aside. Some anal compulsive from bookkeeping or the legal department will take care of them.

Is this arrangement satisfying? If it isn't, feel free to tinker. All problems are pictures and all problems can be resolved by another picture. If you want to diagram your problem and your solution, go ahead. If you want to use fingerpaints, don't let me stop you. You also are not stuck with one arrangement. You can add to it. Maybe the entrails or shreds of your situation as it is don't make a pleasing enough picture even when creatively rearranged. Okay, you're not a one-dimensional being. Add to it from external sources. From your own knowledge, images, and ideas. Mixed media!

In other words, if your problem is ostensibly a marketing problem, perhaps there is some material from finance that could help. Or from MIS. The important thing is the final picture. Not the purity of the elements used. Purity is the last thing you want to worry about.

When you get a picture that you like, you've then got to test it to see if it works. Unfortunately, this is kinetic art. It just doesn't hang on a wall, it has to perform. It can perform weirdly and eccentrically, but it has to actually work. Irrational doesn't mean crazy. It is a method, not an end.

A way to begin testing your picture is to put it into words. Words like paintings have a large irrational umbra to them. A shadow. It's called "connotations." Nonetheless, words, in order to be expressive, follow certain rules—grammar, syntax, semantics.

You have your picture. It seems to work. At least it's not impossible that it could work. It makes you feel good. You're satisfied. Now it's time to describe what you have there.

Strangely enough you'll find that when you attempt to describe even the most eccentric of pictures, the use of words will make the picture sound absolutely rational. When you've finished writing, voila, you've got a report. Nothing is missing and really, all that you need to do is to push all of your craziness into the acceptable format for your organization. Do this. Write up your pictures. Format them. Make them clear and presentable. Then put it aside. After awhile, maybe two weeks if you've got that kind of time, but sufficiently long to get hazy on just what you wrote, go back and read your report. I'll bet you didn't realize just how smart, creative—and rational—you were! It is the answer. You'll recognize that, I'll guarantee you.

Some people are verbal rather than visual. Does this mean that this type of person is unable to tap into his or her irrational functions? Of course not. The same process can occur through verbal means.

Again, you are confronted with a situation that you can't fathom. You know there's a problem, you're expected to act, but you don't have any idea what to do. We've seen what words can do. They have two aspects. First, by putting something into words, you force a structure, grammatical if nothing else, onto the situation. This gives you some measure of control. Second, words, as our earlier exercises have shown, have power. They attract and release energy.

There are two callings in which these two aspects of language are of paramount importance: Magic and poetry. Sometimes, as is the case with Shamanistic religions, the two callings are combined in one person.

When we think of magicians, we think of some guy in a

tuxedo with nothing up his sleeves assisted by the lovely Darla. He's sawing women in half, he's pulling rabbits out of hats. Not a bad way to earn a living. To the more sophisticated, magic becomes "magick" after the psychological and alchemical practices of Aleister Crowley, the eccentric Englishman, poet, mountain climber, chess master, and immensely brilliant, nasty guy.

Crowley in his amusing and insightful way brought the ancient occult and alchemical processes into the modern world—very much like Carl Jung did in the realms of psychiatry. This is not the place to go into a detailed disquisition on the career of Aleister Crowley. For that, a cold, quiet evening, warm fire, glass of sherry and a decent biography, if there is one, would be in order. You'll have great fun and learn something to boot. It is important in our context, however, to recognize what Crowley was doing in his robes and magical instruments. He was "casting spells." Not on the milkmaid down the road or on the state lottery, but on himself. Very much, again, like we are doing. What Crowley was attempting through his practices was to exercise his will on his world. There is nothing particularly bizarre about that. The magical rituals themselves were intended to produce energy and then to direct it toward an end desired by Crowley. Again, we've seen this before. An integral part of these rituals, however, were words of invocation, evocation, and departure. The magical formulas.

Crowley, as we've stated, was a poet. What better person, therefore, to exercise the power of words—and power through words. Think about our usual idea of a magical ceremony. First, there must be protection for the mage. You are calling forces who are of a different order. You have no idea how they will act or why. I've often had a vision that explains this attitude to me. Suppose a Martian were to land on earth. He or she or it is in a room with the greatest scientists in the world. The alien breathes through the pores of its skin and has no nose, ears, or eyes. It is extremely nervous and, unbeknownst to its distinguished interrogator, has its finger or what passes for a finger, wrapped firmly around the trigger of a concealed ray gun. Suddenly, one of the scientists sneezes. The alien freaks and the room is toast.

The same attitude could be said to affect the magician. Hence the formulas of protection. Power is arrayed. Next comes the formulas of invocation. A clear image of the entity called is made in the mind and energies sympathetic to that being are set to vibrating. This also is done through words of power. The words not only have intellectual meaning, but they evoke feelings and vibrate throughout the entire structure of the magician and the physical and psychic area around him or her.

If successful, the being's presence is felt and intuited. This is all that is required. We don't offer an easy chair, fine cigars, and a brandy. The operation, whatever it is, is performed, again releasing power for the magician, and, then the words of dismissal are given. This must be done with exceeding correctness since any mistake here would mean a reversal of polarity in the energy, and, like a spark of lightening jumping at the first available conductor, the magician would be fried. Words once more are used to construct a wall of power.

Why it was so fortunate for his practice that Crowley was a poet is the fact that all poets use words for their vibrational power. The two practices really cannot be separated.

Take as an example Allen Ginsberg's poem "Howl." At the beginning is the invocation, "I saw the best minds of my generation. . . " etc. Then we are introduced at great length to these minds and their situations in the "starry dynamo in the machinery of night." The place and time are created magically through words. But this is not journalism. The words vibrate. Anyone who has been to New York who has ridden up to Harlem, to the El, has seen Ginsberg's "Mohamedan Angels." If you've lived in the city, you have felt the underwater quality of a Bickford's at night. The "city," the entity invoked, grows and vibrates like the magic fetus described in books of alchemy. You take communion with Ginsberg's vision and you overlap your vibrations with his. Is this anything else but sympathetic magic?

There are benighted people in the world who describe poetry as a "craft." The guy who does my plumbing or makes my cabinets works at a craft. This is a view that does violence to the history of both poetry and art in general. Poetry was originally part of religious ceremonies. It could be uttered in a set pattern so that a particular ritual could easily be remembered by the priest, or, it was uttered free-form in a state of ecstacy by a shaman who had purposely altered his or her everyday consciousness so that a magical vision could be induced and a message from the gods transmitted through him or her. The gods spoke fluent poetry, whatever the actual language of the shaman.

The function of the shaman was to receive and transmit messages from the gods. These messages could concern anything from resolving legal disputes to medical cures to foretelling the future—prophesy.

Remember the oracle we visited earlier? Go back, recall what was said to you, and more especially how it was said. Was it a reasoned and scholarly disquisition on the subject matter you presented to it? I'll wager not. Or was it in the form of a rambling, rhythmical, repetitious flow of images that even now evoke an uncomfortably emotional response from you. Such a use of words is poetry.

So when we discuss the use of words in pinning down and directing an unsolvable and unfathomable problem, we are aiming to do poetry.

Now many people will respond that they don't have a poetic bone in their bodies. Well, you have also stated in a rather knee-jerk fashion that you had no intuition. We have seen the falsity of that proposition and I promise you that the idea that you are not a poet is equally false. I am willing to bet the ranch that everyone at some point in their lives, and most likely in adolescence when the sexual energy is at its peak, has written poetry. The emotional renderings of growing so rapidly to physical maturity and, of course, first loves, require a trip into the land of poetry. I am not saying "good poetry," mind you, but that is a relative term anyhow.

Since I recognize that our training and education especially as adults has all been directed towards stomping out both the poetical and magical in us, we will step into poetry like we step into a hot but wonderful bath—slowly.

You're confronted with something. A problem. At work, at home, in yourself. It doesn't matter. The only prerequisite is that it is one that is totally unclear, disquieting and, ostensibly unsolvable as it stares at you, fangs dripping, in your face. The first thing we are going to do with this beast is to suck the blood out of it. We do this by writing prose.

In your most objective frame of mind, or at least as close as you come in your present situation, write a report about this problem. Imagine you are writing this for your boss so think boring. Describe it. Draw any logical inference you can from your description. Discuss the whole thing "rationally." Don't leave anything out, be anal.

By this point you've probably put yourself and the beast facing you to sleep. Look at what you've written. Read it. Have you really solved your problem or simply reduced yourself to narcolepsy? I'm betting on narcolepsy. If you are satisfied, however, *domine, domine, domine*, my work here is done. You're a narcotics addict and there is nothing further I can do with you.

My guess is that the process of writing a report about your problem has not satisfied you, but it has had the effect of calming you down. That is not a bad state in which to be, so let's begin in earnest from here.

At this point we are going to start taking control. We are going to get creative. Take your report. Read it through one more time. Have a cup of coffee with you. Pull out any points that strike you. It doesn't matter if they are the

"main" points, we're not trying to pass a high school literature exam. Jot these points down as you go along. I want you
to take these points, and anything else you care to add, and
write a story about your problems. You can be a character.
You can use fictional characters. You can personify, that is,
make your problem into a person, an animal, a spirit, anything whatever. Make this story as interesting as you can.
Feel free to re-write, but this time, don't get anal.

When you are finished with your story, read it over. By
the way, you can mix media if you like. You may illustrate
your story with drawings. After you have done all of this,
how do you feel? Better than you did after the report, no
doubt. Why? Because now you have invited your irrational
and creative functions to participate in the process. You have
gotten interested on a deeper level. You are no longer simply afraid, now you have the sense that you have some power
behind you. You can feel your own depth and your own psychic solidity.

Let's go on. Many people think that it is the height of art
to produce a "big" work, the thousand-page novel, the
gigantic fresco. We are going to take another tack. We are
going to proceed along Japanese lines, that is, in a minimal-
ist direction. There is a reason for this which we will see
presently.

Take your story and again, jot down the ideas that strike
you. Read through your notes. Now throw them away. Go
about your normal business for a day or so if you have the
time—and you probably have more time than you think if
you are honest with yourself. After you've stewed a bit, recall
all of this to your mind and set about writing a fairly long
poem about it. It can rhyme. It can be free verse. Whatever
form you like. Remember, this is no longer prose so get
"arty." Use words for effect, not just to convey information.
You can babble on, repeat yourself, come up with a catchy
chorus. Have fun. Don't censor! This is only for you. Let it
flow. You probably didn't realize that you were that good!

Watch out, Mr. Ginsberg!

Read your poem several times over the next day or so. Enjoy it more each time. You can punch it up or add to it. It's okay. When you are satisfied with it, put it aside for awhile. Feel good for awhile. Nice respite.

Take your poem out again. Now we are going to compress it. It must fit into twenty lines or less. Why? No particular reason other than that we are now into the alchemical process of distillation. We are going to make a more potent elixir for what ails you.

Reduce. Isn't this much harder than pouring everything out? You don't want to lose anything important, but you do need to purify. You can do anything you have to do to get to twenty lines. Combine things. Eliminate things. Change the form or the rhyme scheme. Anything, but get to twenty lines or less. You're probably not feeling quite so comfortable now, are you? Keep your tension. Don't let it go. As you recall, all of the energy you generate is yours and can be eventually used by you.

Again, take some time to learn to "live" with this poem. Feel the tension it creates. Your unconscious creative facilities are annoyed. They are fully engaged at this point. You are not operating on half your cylinders any more.

It's dirty trick time. We are going to reduce the poem yet again. This time to *tanka* form. The *tanka* is a Japanese poetic form consisting of five lines containing thirty-one syllables. The first line has five syllables, the second line has seven, the third five, the fourth and fifth, seven each. So the pattern is five-seven-five-seven-seven. I am not going to teach you how to break words into syllables, but we'll assume that you have been educated before the recent educational "reforms" and know how this is done.

Take your twenty-line poem and make it into a *tanka*. You want to fully express all that you have observed and felt concerning your experience with your problem. Note, it doesn't have to be explicitly about your problem. It can use an image, a tree, an animal, a cloud, anything, just so long as packed into these thirty-one syllables is everything necessary to express yourself regarding your situation. This could take some time! One starts to appreciate the consummate artistry and discipline of the Japanese poets who forced themselves to express their deepest insights in such a restricted form!

Once you have written your *tanka*, a curious thing has happened, hasn't it? If you are at all successful, the tension you felt when you reduced your long poem to a twenty-line poem has all been sucked into the *tanka!* You are calmer and much more detached from your problem. Enjoy this. Go look at cherry blossoms, or drink green tea. Sit in *seiza* on your rug in a kimono. You sage, you!

Now that you feel comfortable with the spirit of Japanese poetry (okay, I'm exaggerating), we are going to take a final step. We are going to reduce the *tanka* to a *haiku*. A *haiku* is another Japanese form involving the use of seventeen syllables and three lines. The lines go five-seven-five syllables. Take your *tanka*, or rather, the feeling or intuition of your *tanka*, and create a *haiku*. Remember, don't just cut out syllables. Write a whole new poem! Don't lose your feelings or insights, keep them. In fact, as bizarre as it sounds, you can even add to them in this shorter form! Change images if you wish. Go from a cloud to a plum blossom. Or a bottle of pop. Who cares. Just capture in seventeen syllables and three lines, the distilled essence of what you have been cooking all of this time. You now have the elixir, the *Xue*, of your problems under your control and in a safely handled space. Repeat your *haiku*. Enjoy it. Let it vibrate through you. It has more power in seventeen syllables than did any of the stream of words or images or random emotions that you thought were the guts of your problem.

When I say "enjoy" your *haiku*, I mean I want it and you to merge. We've done meditation already in this book. We need to do it again on your *haiku*. This is the quintessence, to use the old alchemical term. It has great power and, you have turned it from a scary, ugly thing into a poem, a thing of beauty. This is the essence of all of the fairy tales from "Beauty and the Beast" to "The Frog Prince" and "The Ugly Duckling." It is the transformation myth. You have worked magic and now you have the magic words. You have correctly handled the problem—so far. The *haiku* is the healing elixir, the magic formula. The first thing you must do with it is to heal yourself. You must cure yourself of your fear and give yourself strength. That is what this magic ritual does for you.

Concentrate on your *haiku*. Become completely familiar with it. Observe every feeling and nuance of feeling that it brings with it. When it is a part of you, you are ready to use it in the real world.

To do this, we must bring the medicine back. We have to dilute it so that it can be used externally. "Just add water," so to speak. This time, however, we are adding pure water, our own water. Unmixed with fear and anxiety and negative emotions. We are adding *aqua vitae*.

To do this we need first to expand the *haiku* on our own terms. Remember how you had to write essays on poems in high school? We are going to do that again. Write a commentary on your *haiku*. Scrape everything you can out of it. Again, don't be critical. If something pops out, it has meaning to you. Additionally, when I say "scrape everything out," of the *haiku*, I don't just mean rational thought but emotional meanings, strong feelings. Interpret these. How do they all connect in these seventeen syllables? Exhaust everything.

When you have your commentary and you are satisfied with it, it is time to re-expand the poem. By this I don't mean to simply repeat the other poems in your first sequence. They are dead. They were simply shadows, ghosts, *kas* as the ancient Egyptians called the spirits of the departed. They were once alive, but are now only shadows of the process we are now on.

We are going to skip the *tanka* in the new process, since while it was helpful to make the jump from the twenty lines to the seventeen syllables less painful, it serves no such purpose on the way out, so to speak. Therefore, expand your *haiku* to twelve lines. Any form. Rhyming, free-verse. The only rule is to keep both the meaning and the feeling of the *haiku*. Of course, you may add ideas, images, and feelings. You may even change the image itself entirely, but you may not lose the energy of the *haiku*.

Once again, write a commentary on your new poem. What does it mean to you by itself? Emotions and resonating images count and should be included. After having looked at it on its own, how does it relate to the *haiku?* Why have you transformed or rather, translated the *haiku* this particular way? Write until you have gotten everything and are satisfied.

One more time, change your twelve-line poem into either a long poem or a story. It is your choice. When you are finished this time, put the result away for a few hours. Don't think about it. Do something mundane and totally practical. Pay your bills. Go to work. Fix the faucet. Then come back to your final poem or short story. Read it over and take out the important points. Write them down. These are headings for an outline. They need to be connected and, in fact, made into a rational, boring, factual outline. Since you have the major headings, connect them in however many steps are necessary to make the outline flow logically and rationally. You now have a plan of approach.

If the outline still leaves you uneasy or confused, make it into a report. Explain it to yourself. Draw a conclusion. You have solved the unsolvable. How do I sitting here without the benefit or the knowledge of your specific problem know this? My question in response is, "How do you feel?" Do you feel satisfied? Do you feel that you want to act? That you are ready to move and get started? Not necessarily on every step of your plan, but at least on the first one or two? If so, the process has been a success. If you can overcome your inertia and actually start, you will find just how appropriate your plan and actions are and you will move to complete the rest of the steps with enthusiasm. Feel free, of course, to adapt and modify as objective data collide with you. That does not invalidate your insights—all plans and activities must be flexible. The fact that you also must be flexible means that you are in the real world, and that is precisely where you have wanted to be since the problem raised its hooded head on your path.

A note about feelings at this point is also in order. I have used feelings as the touchstone of all our exercises so far. Why do I do this? Aren't feelings subjective and untrustworthy? We tend to associate feelings with some sort of weak, effeminate, overly indulgent approach to the real, hard, tough problems of life. In response, I would direct you to our animal heritage and to nature in general. Intellect is a relative late-comer in the cosmos. Life and the various species have survived and flourished for eons before the development of the intellect. Intellect is a wonderful tool, but it is simply one tool among many. This does not denigrate its usefulness, but we also overvalue it at our peril. If you find yourself in the jungle being stalked by a lion, there is a good chance that you, with your superior intellect, are going to be the blue plate special. Do you think that the lion is acting on intellect? Or rather, is he or she acting on instinct? The instinctual protection of territory; an emotional response to invasion? The lion's action, by the way, is entirely correct. If he starts letting too many of these pink monkeys into his territory, the next thing he knows his territory will be Feline Gardens, a golfing community in the heart of the scenic bush with easy access to shopping and entertainment. The lion's feelings are a sure guide to action.

Imagine the human psyche as an amoeba. It puts out appendages to grope its way into the world. To gain information. Four of these appendages are sensation, feeling, thought, and intuition. They are ways of gathering data about the external and internal world. What we are discussing in this book is the situation in which these rational approaches, consisting of sensation—seeing, hearing, touching—and thinking, fail or are lost. Then our other two legitimate human tools, or functions, are intended by nature to be brought into play. Feeling underlies our aesthetic nature, our appreciation of art and the beautiful. Sometimes, nature tells us, the beautiful is closer to truth than the mechanical. The Vermeer is a better picture of reality than the computer program. We use feelings, therefore, as a guide when appropriate. The point is that it is appropriate in far more situations than we have been led to believe.

If feelings are hard for us to fathom and accept, what about intuition? What the hell is that? Perhaps the best way to distinguish feeling from intuition is in terms of speed. Feeling is constant and persists. Intuition is instantaneous. A flash. It's more often than not pictorial, although it may be imageless and take the form of instantaneous and decisive action. An example of the first type of intuition can be found in poetry, in mystical visions, even in science in theory formation as Jung relates in his book *Man and His Symbols*. The best examples of the second are martial arts and Zen *koan* practice. In each, action occurs spontaneously in the impossible situation into which the practitioner has been forced, either by combat on the one hand, or the nonsense problem posed by the Zen Master on the other.

Intuition is an especially useful tool when trying to deal with the Booby Trap problem. This type of problem is recognized by having no good answer. In fact, the more one gets into the problem, the sharper the edges become. Medicine is a fertile ground for these situations. A person has cancer. It is confined to one area but progressing slowly. There is no doubt that if it is left to progress, no matter how slowly, it will eventually kill the person. The growth can be removed surgically, but there is a good chance that opening

85

the body and causing trauma to the area could cause the cancer to spread to the rest of the body and to accelerate its growth on a wider area. What do you do?

Many years ago, I contracted a severe infection. I was hospitalized. If the infection were left to spread, there was a chance of paralysis and blindness. The medication that might arrest the progress of the infection radically suppressed the adrenal glands. This meant that while this particular infection might be cured, I would be open and completely vulnerable to other less exotic infections for the next seven years until my adrenal glands recovered. Nice choice.

Booby Trap problems that come up in parenting are familiar to almost all of us. You want to give your kids a sense of truth and responsibility. You want them to feel self-esteem and that you respect them as persons and that you respect their privacy just as any person would expect. But recently they have been getting odd calls at odd hours from people you don't know. Their moods swing radically. They seem particularly secretive about where they are going when they go out, and about that box in their room. They have on more than one occasion threatened to leave home because you don't trust them. Once they even tried and almost left the state. Of course, as all parents know, if children are successful in getting away, you may never see them again. You may never know what has happened to them. As a prosecutor I have met the nice middle-class parents of more than one murdered prostitute. Parenting presents the toughest problems of all since the emotional content and the closeness of these problems are nuclear in their potential for devastation.

Needless to say, reason is not often a trustworthy guide in these situations and is more than likely on the level of a sick joke. Feelings, too, become too intense, short-circuiting the normal channels. Here we hope for inspiration. That is the function of intuition.

You can wait patiently for your intuition to flash while

drinking Maalox and gin cocktails in the wee hours of the night or, you can, as with the feeling function, invite it in.

We could proceed as in the Nebulous type of problem and write things out. To do this however would be to miss the essence of the problem, which is its contradictions. These contradictions need to be preserved because they contain the energy of the problem. To represent an inherently contradictory problem as a smooth surface would be inaccurate and, would waste the energy of the problem rather than let it be used for your own ends. The problem needs to be represented in all of its maddening fullness. To begin by writing the problem out would be to force a grammatical structure on it and would thus defeat the purpose.

Instead, we will begin non-verbally with a drawing. Sit down with any materials you desire; crayons, colored pencils, pastels, paints, or any combination of these. Think a bit about your problem, but do it in a "off-center" sort of way. Do not meditate! Do not attempt to find a rational solution, that is, don't actually think. Although of the two, this is one instance in which meditation would be worse.

When I say look at you problem "off-center," I mean this in the same spirit as a Zen archer looks at his target. He doesn't really look at his target, but he is aware of the target and where it is. He simply draws his bow and shoots. A master hits the target every time. The master, after all, is superior to the hunk of straw that encompasses the target. In other words, don't "concentrate" on the problem, but allow it to seep into your consciousness.

When you feel that you are ready, draw your problem. It can and should be as jangling to the nerves as the problem itself. Use contrasting, clashing colors if you like, or, soft, cloud-like pastels, which show the situation as vague and ungraspable. Draw figures or do a complete abstract. The important thing, just as with a Japanese poem, is not how it presents itself to you objectively, but how you react to it. The intensity of your reaction is the important thing here. It is with your emotional reaction that you must be satisfied.

When you have completed a drawing that satisfies you as to its genuineness as a non-verbal representation of your problem, it is time to become verbal again. You need now to write a description of your drawing. Not of your problem, but of your drawing. Describe this in any way you wish. It should, however, be a description and not a story. It also should not be a report. Just describe what you see and what you feel. Describe what it is in the drawing that makes you feel a certain way and tell yourself why this aspect of your drawing elicits this particular response from you.

We are going to proceed in a very Japanese fashion as we work with this particular type of problem. You may roll the problem around in your mind as much as you like before you begin to put it down in your drawing. Just like a Japanese ink drawing, however, once you start your drawing you may not go back and alter either it or your thoughts. The same holds true with your description and any other step in this particular process. Once begun and then completed, that is it as your intuition has given it to you. If, when you have completed the entire process, you are not completely comfortable, you can start the process over from the beginning, although you must be aware of the fact that you will not then be following the same intuition, but a wholly new and different one. Of course, there is nothing wrong with this and I encourage you to do it if that is what you feel is necessary. I just want you to be aware of the distinction between this process and the function it follows and the other processes we have previously utilized.

When you are satisfied with your description of your drawing, it is time to combine both the drawing and the verbal description into a sort of halfway house—a diagram. I am not going to tell you how to do your diagram. You can do it like a flow chart with arrows, or you can do it with connecting lines. Whatever. What you want is a schematic skeleton, a map, of your drawing and what you've said about it. You may put in words or short phrases at key points since this is a diagram not a drawing. The goal is that, as with all diagrams, you should be able to comprehend everything that went into your drawing and your description at a glance.

Become comfortable with your diagram. There it all is! You comprehend everything in one shot. Mull this diagram over for a day or so. It has a calming influence because for once you have every aspect in one place. At least you can see everything now. It is less scary that way. No surprises.

After you thoroughly "know" your diagram we are going to transform it into a format that is not simply a picture. While the diagram is useful, it is static. The problem is not. The diagram was used as a sedative only, not as a solution.

Take the elements of your diagram and use them to write a nonsense story. While it is a legitimate short story (emphasis on short), it is like a fairy tale in that it should not make a lot of sense. No phony moral. You should be entertained but scratching your head at the end. The thing to avoid here is a solution or a conclusion. Nonetheless, reading your nonsense story should be fun. The object is confusion and a laugh.

Again, give yourself some time to let your head clear out and the story gel in your mind, then, rewrite the story in one paragraph. Try to make the paragraph amusing for you. You're not on stage in Las Vegas, but try to make the paragraph make you smile. Make the paragraph as close to a joke as you can. It can have a punchline, but not a conclusion. I know that this is difficult. Comedy is much harder than tragedy. Most of us have been taught that life is hard and tragic and have internalized this. We have no sense of humor. I'm telling you that life is hard, very hard—and funny beyond belief.

Remember Frank the CEO we spoke about earlier? The guy who fired my friend and a lot more like him? Well, Frank, because he was so young when he took over his company, tried to earn the respect of the older executives by "dressing old." He would wear baggy, dark suits and Clark Kent hats, to "look old." What an idiot! Surely there are quite a few laughs in this at old Frank's expense! Humor is everywhere. Do you think that the gods could ever create a Hitler without the dopey mustache? They don't work that way.

If you're having trouble writing a joke or at least something amusing, look around you a bit. What makes you laugh or at least start to laugh before your adult mind tells you to "stop fidgeting"? Enjoy this. Encourage it. Then write your joke. Nobody said it had to be good. Look at Henny Youngman—he made a very lucrative career out of bad jokes!

Enjoy your joke. You've earned it. When you feel a bit better, we are ready for another step. We are again going to get Japanese. Put on your kimono, sit in *seiza*, green tea at the ready. Take your joke and reduce it to one line. Try to keep the contradictoriness and humor of all your previous work. This one-liner is your Zen *koan*.

A koan is a nonsense sentence or question that is posed to a Zen student by his *roshi* or master. Examples are "What is the sound of one hand clapping?" Or, "What did your face look like before you were conceived?" These *koans* are the methods, the keys that are used to snap the Zen student into enlightenment.

You may look at these examples of Zen *koans* and conclude that they are nothing like what we are presently doing. We are using a long, painstaking process to solve a serious problem. However, such an assessment is plain wrong. These Zen one-liners are the culmination of a process that has "boiled down" all of the Buddhist teachings—and there are thousands of volumes to the Buddhist corpus—from the time of the Buddha, through all of his followers, ecclesiastical conferences, and commentaries over centuries in India and China. All of Buddhism, a system that attempts to grapple with the ultimate and all-encompassing problems of human and universal existence, is included in these single-lined nonsense statements. And you thought your problem was tough!

Boil your joke down to one line. This is your *koan*. The object of the *koan* is to so fry your mind, to so block-up your energy that your intuition will explode. This explosion is your enlightenment. Get it?

When you have your *koan*, you can go no further. Now you must roll it around like those Chinese medicine balls that you see at the health food stores. Here is also where neither I nor anyone else can help you. I can't even tell you whether your meditation or your handling of your *koan* will be fun or painful or frustrating. I can tell you, however, that if and when the explosion occurs for you, you will not get an "answer." What you will get is an impulse to act and a "way" to act. This "way" is your *do*. The term *do* comes from the Chinese term *dao*. In Japanese, the term *do* is added to other words to indicate a certain approach to life. Examples are judo, kendo, karatedo, chando. *Judo* and *karatedo* are probably familiar to you. *Kendo* is the way of the sword. *Chando* is the way of tea. There are *dos* for flower arranging and for being a government bureaucrat. Each *do*, however, is, in the end, individual. This is because all enlightenment is individual. Your do comes from your *koan*, which comes from your unique life with its custom-tailored, unique problems. When you get the impulse to act, act. Don't think, act.

In the movie, *The Good, the Bad and the Ugly*, Eli Wallach plays a Mexican bandit. He is soaking in a bathtub when an enemy barges in, six-shooter drawn. The enemy has Wallach trapped, as he sneeringly cocks the hammer on his gun. Then the idiot begins to tell Wallach how much he hates him and how he is going to enjoy killing him. Wallach, who has a gun hidden under the soapsuds, simply shoots the fool. As the thug crumples and dies, Wallach states, "If you're going to shoot, shoot. Don't talk. Shoot." Same advice. Once your intuition tells you to act and gives you a way, don't question it—act.

In this chapter we have discussed what I consider the most prevalent types of problems facing us; those in which we have only two obligations, not only the obligation of coming up with an answer, but also of actually framing the question. The important point to remember about these types of problems is that although they have their roots in the "real world" and their solutions ultimately must apply to this world, these problems are inherently irrational and no help whatsoever can or will come from "objective" sources either in the external world or in the "rational" parts of your mind. It is because of this that the irrational functions of your mind must be engaged and trusted to serve you as they have been designed by nature to do. Fortunately we have many examples of processes that use these functions of feeling and intuition. Most obvious, of course, is art. Religion, however, especially those religions which utilize meditation, also tap the energies of these functions. Zen Buddhism is the quintessence of these practices. That these methods are useful in the so-called practical world can obviously be witnessed by the place of Japan, the nation that refined Zen practice, in our modern financial and political world.

In the next chapter I want to refine our techniques for framing problems and answers. Basically we will be dealing with analogy and metaphors. These are poetic concepts, but by now you must be aware of just how often poetry has a place in even the most hard-headed and practical of lives. We are not machines. Machines have plugs. Human beings don't.

In the final two chapters we will deal more directly with action itself, the point where we ended this chapter.

CHAPTER FOUR | # What's It Like?

As I've said earlier, my father was a football coach. Like
with many other careers, this meant a good deal of moving
around when he was starting out. His first job was at a place
called Cherry Tree High School in a place named, consistently enough, Cherry Tree, Pennsylvania. Don't let the
bucolic name fool you, however; Cherry Tree was smack in
the middle of the Western Pennsylvania coal fields, and
football in that area has a meaning that nobody from the
outside can ever begin to fathom. Between the handing of
the Keys to the Kingdom to St. Peter and the return of
Christ on a cloud—there is only football.

My father managed to steal eleven or twelve kids from
the mines and since football beat the hell out of crawling in
a coal pocket in water up to your chest for ten hours in the
dark with no human contact, he had guys whose beef was
laced with a huge dose of desperation. They had several
championship seasons. On the basis of this record, my father
was hired to coach all athletics at Newport High School in,
where else, Newport, Pennsylvania.

Newport was located in the hills of Central
Pennsylvania. Now, when most people think of Pennsylvania
they think of a bustling east coast state. They think of

Philadelphia. They think urban, or, if they've been there for a visit, they think of the flat, manicured fields of the Amish, the commercialized skiing of the Poconos or, the old colonial towns on what was the King's Highway in the southeastern part of the state. The bulk of Pennsylvania, however, is nothing like that. Once you cross the Susquehanna River, you are in the woods. Hence the name: Penn-Sylvania, Penn's Woods. When I was a boy, we were entertained every year by at least one story of bear hunters getting lost in the wilds of Western Pennsylvania. Sometimes they were found dead.

Newport was hidden away in the foothills of the Alleghenies. It was a river town on the shores of the Juniata River. In the remote past it did not look to the Quakers and Redcoats in Philadelphia. This region turned to Fort Duquesne and its French garrison and fur traders. In fact, when I was growing up, and I'll wager to this day, it was commonplace to see stretched hides drying on farm walls in the winter and fall.

But Newport was a step up from Cherry Tree, which itself, was pretty urbane in its own corner of Cambria County.

There were three things to do in Newport in the late forties and early fifties—athletics, boozing, and fishing. (Actually four. Hunting was bigger than all of the other three and had the added joy of combining alcohol with firearms.) My father, as stated, was the head of all the athletics of Newport, so he drank free at all the local watering holes—and there were a surprisingly large number of these in this small town that before global warming often got socked in with foot after foot of snow starting about October every year. My father was also a fisherman. In short, he fit right into Newport society.

We lived literally right next to the river in an ancient and very scary dried-blood red brick building that had been the former Presbyterian parsonage. Water snakes used our basement for shedding their skins and my mother often found dried snake skins in among her canned goods. She was forever killing these critters in our yard with her trusty iron rake.

In the off-season, my dad would disappear through the back yard and over the railroad tracks (did I mention that we had railroad tracks in our back yard?) and down to the Juniata with his friends, newly returned from deer season or pheasant season or rabbit season or whatever was on the block at that time of year (mighty good eatin' though) and fish for bass or catfish or whatever else was still in that wild river before progress fixed its acid content for good.

After the dishes and any other chores she had—this was the fifties after all—my mother and I and our dog, a huge black and white mongrel named Nippy, would make the trek through the yard and the snakes to the river bank.

Of course, this was a men's only club amid the beer bottles next to the railroad embankment, but my mom, scarf on her head, rake in one hand, boy child in the other, fresh from squashing a copperhead, was not about to be told where she could go. So we would annoy my dad and his friends, the bluebloods of Newport, Pennsylvania, by watching them fish.

Which brings us to the point of all of this. One of my earliest memories is of a spring night when we were watching my dad's fishing exploits. It was starting to get dark and the train on the tracks across the river already had its light on. As the smell of its soot drifted in the cold breeze across the river, my dad got a hard strike on his line. His friends wobbled to their feet among the rolling and tinkling beer bottles, since it had been a slow night.

The excitement grew as the rod bent. This thing must be a lunker. Probably a river cat. Or a bullhead. It had to be a catfish. If it was a bass—too early for them—but if it was a bass, it would be a record breaker!

The anticipation grew. Our dog became agitated, running up and down the bank. The thing had still not broken the surface. Probably not a bass then, since bass came rapidly to the top and put on a show fighting for every inch of line. Probably a catty, and judging from the tension on the line, this thing would feed us for a week—if the line didn't break!

A massive shape just poked through the surface. Since it was almost dark, nobody could make it out. A black dome rose out of the water. A bullhead! And judging from the diameter of its head, the biggest anyone had ever seen! My father was smirking. He was in masculine, chest-hair heaven. My mother was batting her eyelashes. The other men were batting their eyelashes. And then, about three yards from shore it hit us—a stench that at once combined the subtle bouquets of wet feces and fermented sweat socks. A yard from shore we could all see that firmly attached for all eternity to my father's line was a genuine Juniata River Stinkpot Turtle! These were created by God originally as added torments for the souls of the damned but somehow escaped the fourth pit of hell and made it to the Juniata. They were the ugliest, meanest, and as a pièce de résistance, smelliest creatures this side of hell.

The beast's red eyes glowed with the fires of Hades. My mother, finishing a swig of my father's beer decided that being a John Ford heroine, one of the guys, had somehow lost its appeal. Jean Arthur wouldn't hang around a Stinkpot Turtle either. She took my hand and her trusty rake and headed off over the railroad tracks to Stately Reptile Manor. My father and his friends scratched themselves and tried to figure how to get this little beauty off the hook. I can only assume that they did.

Sometimes life is good. Just like sitting on a river bank with your good friends, fanned by an early spring breeze, with two cold six-packs at the ready. You're the head of marketing. You've been in your job for a year. No complaints. The president personally hired you and you have even been invited to his home with your wife. The numbers are good. The staff likes you. Even the vice-president and chief operating officer, J. Stinkpot Turtle seems to like you, even though he wasn't involved in the decision to hire you. At least he's always smiling at you. Funny, though, you never do see his teeth. Oh well.

Your buddy the president goes on vacation. A nice break for everyone. But one night as you're leaving you see some strange BMWs and Lexuses in the parking lot. You bump into a woman you know to be a member of the board of directors. She's nervous. You glance up at the office windows of Stinkpot Turtle and the blinds are pulled. Hmm.

It comes back to you that your head of copywriting, your number two man, has been having lunch with Stinkpot Turtle. Oh well, they both like to play chess. You've seen the board when you've walked by the room. Nothing to worry about. Things are fine. The numbers are okay—aren't they? Maybe you could have closed the Parkinson deal. Nah. I worked my butt off on that one. Then again, if I had had the Society American stats, but copywriting said that research said that the stats weren't ready. Too bad. Might have helped. Oh well, can't blame me. I mean, surely, they can't blame me?

The next day J. Stinkpot Turtle is in your office. Waiting. He's smiling. Damn! This time you get to see his pearlies in all their capped glory. Uh, the board met last night. Uh, they don't think it's necessary to contact the blissfully vacationing president. They'll talk to him later. Uh. You know, uh, we're not really happy about the Parkinson account. In fact, we've reviewed all of your deals in the last year, uh, I got them from copywriting, uh, that's not important, but, uh, we're, me and the board that is, are pretty disappointed. Uh, security will be here soon. We'll pack up for you. Uh. Jim from copywriting will be filling in for you. No. We'll box up the pictures of your wife and kids. By the way, uh, we can only authorize four weeks severance. Ah. Security is here. Sorry.

Same turtle. Different venue.

You're the head of a heavy machinery plant in Stuttgart. You look out at the sun shining on the snow, whistle some Schubert, mutter some Goethe. Der Herr Gott ist zehr gut!

Five years ago when you were a salesman, you sold a metal stamping machine to an American company in Indiana. Being German, your company insisted on proper installation and dispatched an engineer to oversee the installation of the machinery. He arrives at the plant and inspects the machine which has been plunked down on the cement floor right next to the windows. A pad comes out. He begins to scribble numbers feverishly. He starts to curse under his breath in German—which by the way is incredibly effective—and then orders the nearest shop person to get the manager, one J. Stinkpot Turtle. He informs Stinkpot Turtle that the floor is not stable enough to resist the intense vibrations of the machine. He pulls out the manual, nicely translated into English, that clearly explains where the machine should be placed. Stinkpot Turtle shrugs. The engineer explains that the machine will eventually weaken the floor and someone could get seriously injured. Stinkpot Turtle myopically, and typically, is mesmerized by his division's bottom line. He isn't moving anything. It's just fine where it is. The engineer tries again. No go. He packs his briefcase and marches directly out of the plant and onto a plane for Stuttgart.

Your company sends a letter disavowing the sale and demanding that the machinery be returned. It refuses to install it, clearly citing all of the safety hazards involved. Stinkpot Turtle does not even deign to respond and hires Larry, Darryl, and Darryl to install this marvel of German engineering.

Last week the concrete floor crumbled as predicted and the machine crashed to the sub-basement killing three men and two women, one pregnant, and injuring a dozen others. The families have all filed suit against the plant. Mr.

Stinkpot Turtle is now president of another division and is not named in the suit. On your desk, however, this fine morning is a letter from your attorney advising you that you and your firm and the engineer have been named as third-party defendants in the pending suit. Himmel!

Sometimes you just don't know that there's a problem. You've done all of the right things. Who would know, after all, that Stinkpot Turtles also like bass bait? We've all been blind-sided by ugly situations at times when we thought things were going just fine and we believed ourselves at peace with our lives and the world. The company decides to downsize. The kid gets arrested. The EPA finds toxic waste buried on the rural getaway property you bought. All of this out of the blue. No warning. No clues.

Like the Juniata River, life presents a surface and depths. Sometimes you can see agitation on the surface and guess that there are rocks or other obstacles on the bottom. At other times, the river can be quite deceptive; smooth and placid on the surface with snags or nests of snakes or—turtles of less than savory aroma—lurking underneath. It is, of course, a trite metaphor, but to navigate the river—in this case your own river—it is absolutely necessary to know that river.

Recently, my wife and my youngest son and I went to an event called Tallstacks in Cincinnati. Tallstacks is the largest gathering of steamboats in the United States. There on the banks of the Ohio River on what used to be the wharf district are dock after dock of paddle-wheelers. Some are no bigger than excursion boats and others, like the Mississippi Queen, remind one of the Imperial Destroyer at the beginning of *Star Wars*. Seeing this magnificent boat steam down the Ohio literally takes your breath away. Behind you the wharf area has been painted with shop fronts to resemble the old Cincinnati of riverboat days. At that time, flat-bottomed steamboats paddled from Pittsburgh down past Cincinnati to St. Louis, Memphis, Vicksburg, and eventually New

Orleans. It was the time Mark Twain memorialized and, if you've read Mark Twain, you know well that in order to pilot one of these floating palaces you had to know all about the largest inland water system in North America. You spent years learning its shoals, currents, depths, sandbars, and rocks. Only a master could be entrusted with such glory. We must become pilots, we must know our own rivers.

Water is a curious thing. It holds a special fascination for all creatures but especially human beings. I don't think there is anyone who cannot appreciate being beside water—from the Atlantic or Pacific which stretch beyond all horizons to a shack by the smallest mid-Ohio mud hole. Water calms. Water heals. Water is an aid to meditation. It makes us think.

When we are suddenly hit by the unexpected problem, we must react to it just like any other problem. If we are very lucky, the problem is clearly drawn and its solutions stand in clear relief and the problem-solving techniques which we have developed so far can be used to meet them. However, as we have seen in the previous chapter, this often is not the case and our problem is vague and undefined. Naturally, we now have techniques for handling even these types of problems. But the situations we are now approaching may be even less defined and less readily apparent. Like the head of marketing on the eve of his firing in our example, we may simply be faced with a vague feeling of unease. Of course, by now we have recognized the paramount importance of feelings and know they are intended by nature as a survival mechanism, early warning in this case, so we must take them seriously and tune in to their messages.

Again, however, like the Stinkpot Turtle, its shell may only be visible as a dark blotch under the surface, or a black hump halfway out of the water, or, fully exposed. The less exposed, the more difficult and the more dangerous it is for us. It also presents us with far more opportunities if captured at an early stage than if we wait for it to enter our lives fully armed and on dry land.

The less developed a problem is, the less defined, the more potential energy is bound in it. The more potential for us. Once a problem starts unfolding in your life, it releases energy—at you. Utilizing our previous techniques, we can use this energy for our own purposes, but why should we waste any of it? It is extremely important to be sensitive to the energy content of our life. Energy, as we have seen, and as the ancient *Qigong* Masters and Zen Masters have taught us, is what determines the quality of our lives. The trick is to grab and use as much as we can. We do not steal, however, we accept. Problems offer us energy. It is a Zen joke for those who can appreciate it.

As I've said, our feelings are our usual guide to a potential problem, but our intuition may also give us a flash, illuminating like lightning things hidden from view. The point is to develop the sensitivity of these functions so that our early warning system exceeds NORAD (which may not be all that difficult). The earlier we perceive a potential disturbance in our river, the better able we are to deal with it and, the more energy and potential we can derive and use from it. The intuited or nascent problem therefore, becomes a buried treasure rather than the sea monster we first thought it to be.

How do we exercise our feelings and intuition? Just like our muscles or our brains, by using them. We have already been doing this in the previous chapters, but now we must extend it almost into the range of the paranormal. We must develop *siddhis* or occult powers. Neat, huh?

When trying to discover hidden problems, like those facing our marketing manager or our engineer from Stuttgart, what we want to do first is to get a glimpse beneath the surface of our lives, to make out some of the shapes gliding around down there. We are going to do this from two angles; from the surface itself and then from beneath the waves. Since the world down there will be strange to us, we probably will have very little idea what we are dealing with. The next step then, will be to "bait" these things into entering our world. There is a scene at the end of the Fellini film, *La Dolce Vita*, where a giant sea monster has been washed up on the shore and beached. The creature lies there, an amorphous blob, gasping for breath and obviously dying. The creatures that we entice out of our depths can also behave that way, or, they can adapt and become amphibians or dinosaurs. Strangely, it would be better for us if they became Brachiosaurs rather than fish and chips. While fish and chips are less threatening, they have so much less potential than Brachiosaurs.

Once the creature–the hidden problems or threats in our lives—has been coaxed onto the land, it must be netted and tamed so that we can use it like any other domestic animal. A note, however, a domestic animal is still an animal. Don't forget that.

Our tools for the second part of this procedure will be, as stated in the last chapter and in the Introduction, analogies, metaphors, and similes. But at the moment, we are going to indulge in the ancient art of scrying.

Scrying is sometimes called crystal gazing, that is, looking into a crystal ball. While this is the most familiar of the techniques of scrying, other articles such as mirrors or bowls of water have also been used. The idea is to gaze intently at the crystal surface without blinking until the optic nerves are neutralized and hypnogogic visions begin to appear in depths of the ball, mirror, or water. Hypnogogic visions are similar to the colored pictures our minds make just before we fall asleep. We start with random blotches of color—purple, yellow, orange—and then begin to form pictures as we become more relaxed. We slide from these pictures into dreams and we are asleep.

Since we have been using a metaphor already in this chapter, that of a river, or at least a body of water—choose your own—we will use water as our method of scrying. We are going to scrye together now; not to predict the future, not yet, but to "see" and get acquainted with the shapes and figures gliding about under the surface of our lives, hidden from our normal view.

Let's go back to our trusty quiet place. Be exotic. Wear a robe or a kaftan or silk pajamas. Something that is out of the ordinary, that makes you feel unusual. For this exercise you do not need absolute quiet. For once you can put on the New Age tapes, or some form of Asian music, sitar, koto, or even oud. Gamelin is also nice, especially the Javanese variety. Your choice, anything to make you feel odd.

While you can use incense or other scents, too, you might want to be careful about that. What we are actually doing is just inside the border of ceremonial magic and certain scents have affinities with certain, uh, shall we call them, "beings." While I can't tell you whether the entities are "real" in the same sense as your postman is real, or whether they are figments of your imagination, in energy terms, they are quite real and not all of them are folks you would willingly invite to Thanksgiving dinner, if you get my drift. So be careful with scents. Research them or use something very neutral or be safe and forget them altogether.

At any rate, you are in silk pajamas, you feel different, you are in your quiet place and the slow, deep Javanese gongs are vibrating in the background. Since the directions concerning traditional scrying are confusing and, quite frankly, contradictory, I am going to arbitrarily pick my own choice concerning how this is done.

Do your scrying at night. The room should not be totally dark, but a soft, low light should be used; a candle or a very small watt bulb. I turn on the light in the hall outside my den and use the light from under the door for illumination.

This time also, I want you to sit a certain way; in *seiza*. *Seiza* is the Japanese meditation posture, but I'm using it because I think it will allow your head to tilt slightly forward so as to give you more of a feeling of "gazing."

Seiza is simply kneeling on the floor and sitting your butt on the back of your legs. Do this on a rug or folded towel or other soft surface. In my karate classes we are required to sit in *seiza* on a bare wooden floor. It is exceedingly uncomfortable and will distract you from your concentration. Your feet can be pointed backwards or bent at angles to each other. The important thing is to avoid cramping. Experiment until you find what is comfortable for you and don't be afraid to change your posture or "fidget" if you get uncomfortable.

Traditional scrying is done with the eyes open. Here, however, we are going to close our eyes. The surface we are examining is not some glass ball, but our lives. The images will come just as they do every night before sleep. This time, however, we will examine them.

Having said this, don't let me discourage you from using a crystal ball or mirror or pan of water if you so desire. There are, as I have said many times, no good reasons to limit yourself.

In *seiza*, the back is usually held straight as is the head. Here, however, I want you to lean slightly forward and imagine that you are looking at an object about a foot to two feet in front of your knees. This object is a pool of water. The surface is as still as glass and reflects the stars and the slightly luminous wisps of clouds overhead. In fact, without the edges of the pool, you could not tell whether you were viewing the sky or the water.

Stretch your arms out to your sides, but slightly in an arc like you were holding a huge ball. This will give you an idea of how big your pool is. It can be as large or small as you like, but it shouldn't be too large or you will lose control or at least be unable to see everything and, it should not be too small or you won't be able to "catch" much.

When you've gotten an idea of the size of your pool, place your palms on your upper thighs and relax your arms. Let your breathing slow naturally as you've done so many times before. Keep "looking," however. "Watch" anything that comes into view behind you eyes. As you are watching these things appear—clouds, pastel fogs, and mists—try to see behind them into the pool. Can you see the bottom? How deep is it? The depths will vary with your state of mind and life situations. It will vary with what you are allowed to see and with what your inner infinity wants to show you.

Like the colors before you sleep, the mists will start to form shapes, sea creatures gliding or hovering or simply sitting still on the bottom. This is a trip to the aquarium. What do you see? I am not asking you to put a name on anything you see. If you knew the names of your sea creatures, you would already know what you were dealing with and there would be no need for all of this. Restrain yourself. Relax. Don't jump to names. Instead, describe. What do you see? Not "what" in the sense of a label, but in the sense of patterns, colors, actions, connections. What do you see under the surface? Remember your visions.

Since you are peering into a strange world, what you see may at first appear distorted to you. It may make you feel uncomfortable. But watch these creatures. They are sea creatures, lighter than the fluid surrounding them. They can travel and move with a type of grace that we on the hard surface of our day-to-day world can barely imagine. Watch their arcs and rolls and dives. The water makes them glow like gems or precious metals. Gems and minerals are of both the earth and the water. They are things of great beauty and they are from the depths.

At this point simply enjoy your vision, but also remember what you see. When you are thoroughly relaxed and have spent some time in these depths, enough to feel a sense of comfort and awe, start to rise to the surface. Draw your vision back behind your eyes. Awaken once again inside your own head. Orient yourself, then open your eyes. Do not move right away. Come back.

When you are again in your room, but before you are totally into your everyday consciousness, before you totally feel "normal," write down what you saw, that is, describe the creatures and things you observed under the surface. Their shapes, colors, types of movement. Where you first saw them and where they went. How they got there, and finally, how you felt about them.

Why did you feel that way? As you observed them, did your feelings change? How? How do you feel about them right now? What characteristics of these creatures struck you most forcefully? Color? Why? Shape? Why? Speed? Why? Was there one who especially captured your attention? Why? You may even draw these creatures. Use color. Be sure to get all of the emotional tone as well as the "objective" facts about the creatures into your drawings. Again, put all of this away for a day or so. Breathe air again. Drink coffee. Go to work. Wait until you feel "normal" again.

Take out your descriptions and your drawings. How does "seeing" these things again make you feel? Can you tell yourself why? Do any of these creatures mean anything to you? What I mean by this is; do you feel some connection between the creature and anything in your normal, everyday life? If so, what is the connection? It is exceedingly important here that you don't censor. Write down this connection just as it is given to you. As you know, you are talking to these creatures. You are the link between two worlds.

At this point you may well ask "What in the world does this have to do with anything?" Let's return to our marketing director. He had a sense of unease every time he saw the vice-president, Stinkpot Turtle, right? His sense of unease seemed baseless. This "sense" or feeling of unease, however, was the survival mechanism of his feeling function trying to warn him that there was a threat from Stinkpot Turtle. If he had responded to his feelings he could have begun to accumulate clues to the nature of this threat. He noticed that Turtle was meeting with the head of copywriting. Why would the vice-president be meeting regularly with the marketing director's underling? What was going on?

Obviously, from this example, the marketing director was not privy to the corporate shake-up being plotted by Stinkpot Turtle. He would, therefore, have no way of knowing the exact steps Turtle would take, but, being alerted by his feelings of unease, he could have tried to intuit or get some sense of the shape of the threat so that he could make some defensive moves. One that is obvious is to call his friend the vacationing president. If not immediately, at least before the clandestine board meeting.

The point is that what we are doing in this exercise is not simply viewing pretty sea creatures, but using the creatures we see as symbols of hidden forces operating in or under our day-to-day lives. The eventual connection with our everyday lives is, therefore, of paramount importance. The trick at this initial viewing stage, however, is to let these creatures reveal themselves. It is only later, after we step back, that we do the crucial work of linking these creatures to our surface life. That is the stage we are at now.

Is there something about the connection of your creature or creatures with your everyday life that you've missed, that raises something unusual about that part of your life? What is it? Does knowing this information brought by your sea creature help you in any way with this aspect of your life? Do you know something now that you didn't see or know before? Can you use this information? If so, how? If you can't see how at this moment, but there is a strong emotional or intuitive charge to this idea, let it stew for a few days. It might well need a bit more time to come to the surface. You could even visit it again by using the same procedure, but I would allow a bit of time to elapse before doing that.

Being back in the "real" world, and with a fresh catch from the sea, if there is, as there probably will be, some confusion about just what you have, you can always make bouillabaisse. That is, you can use the exercises we developed in chapter 3 to help you define what you have. It might, however, be good to leave some of your catch back in the sea. This doesn't mean that you let them hide and have power over you, but rather, you keep their living energy in your pool for your enjoyment and use. You feed them regularly, clean the water and do not feel threatened anymore because it's your pool and you can see them clearly any time you wish.

Since the purpose of these exercises in this chapter is to sensitize you to processes in your life taking place under the surface, and to thus help you deal with problems before they poke their dorsal fins above the waves and rush at you with jaws wide open, and since we stated that this might very well involve the development and use of *siddhis* or occult powers, we are now going to take our exercise a step further and read the future. This is scrying, after all.

The point of scrying is to see what will or can happen. Now, looking into the future is like looking at anything from a distance. The exact contours of an object might not be visible, but some idea of its nature probably can be determined. I remember the Lone Ranger from television when I was a boy. The Lone Ranger would be on a ridge. Off in the distance, miles away, he would see something. Dust rising from the plains. The bad guys were coming. Their horses were raising clouds of dust. The Lone Ranger couldn't tell exactly how many bad guys there were, but he did know that there were too many for him! With this knowledge, he could also come up with a plan. Maybe he could get his rifle and hide in the rocks. Maybe he could hop on Silver and ride away as fast as he could.

A nonfiction example of how reading the future could head off the bad guys is our friend the German engineer. How in the world could this guy have foreseen this seemingly unexpected lawsuit? Again, there were clues, and again, the engineer's solution of believing that his moral pronouncements to a man like Stinkpot Turtle and his simple retreat to Germany would somehow absolve him of any further connection with his company's machine sitting squarely on the floor of Turtle's plant was naïve, to say the least.

The engineer was working for a firm that made international sales. He was doing business in the United States, a country notorious for its litigiousness. It is a well-known tactic of American tort defense law firms to try to bring in third-party defendants when faced with personal injury suits to spread both the blame and the liability. Anyone doing business in this environment should know that simply shutting a briefcase and walking off does not necessarily end things. In this sense, our engineer is even denser and in a deeper state of denial than our marketing director. The marketing director did have feelings of unease. There were clues that he noted. He chose, however, not to respond. The engineer, on the other hand, took the imperious attitude that his word was law, allowed no access to his feelings, and refused to entertain any clues from his confrontation with Mr. Turtle that future litigation could be a possibility. If the engineer had accepted or considered the bad feelings stemming from this confrontation over the improper use of his machine, drawn from his experience of doing business in the United States, and then projected the possibilities of this legal environment and this confrontation into the future, he may have been able to at least alert his legal team and preempt any litigation.

Perhaps a few words are necessary to convince you that you can, in fact, read the future or, as will be seen in chapter 5, a certain type of future. You didn't believe me about a lot of things so far, such as your ability to get in touch with your feelings, your power to use intuition, your artistic and poetic capabilities. But if you've done the exercises, you've discovered many abilities you didn't know you had. I can assure you that if you are as open as you were when trying the other activities, you will also be able to read the future.

How is this possible, you may ask. We need to go back again to your position in the universe. You are the gate between two infinities; two worlds. One is what we by convention call the "external" world although we now know that this term has almost no meaning except to contrast it with the other infinity, the "internal" world; the world of Freud's personal unconscious and Jung's collective unconscious. As the gate, you have access to either world. You know this since you've been to both many times.

The external world is subject to a certain type of physics. That is, objects in this world have certain types of relationships with each other. Gravity is an example of one of these relationships. The Newtonian laws of motion are others. So are the actions in a cloud chamber, the cyclotron, and the probabilistic equations of Einstein and Heisenberg. In a restricted sense, the external world is structured along three spatial dimensions and a fourth dimension, time. It is impossible to tell, however, whether all of these dimensions "exist in our minds," or, whether they are really "out there" in nature. Anyone doubting this needs only open Kant's *Critique of Pure Reason*. I won't repeat his arguments here. Needless to say they suck all of the air out of the idea of an external world. It is not place, but the quality of the relationships existing in a "world" that differentiate one world from another.

Since time exists in only one of the two worlds we are discussing, when we read the future, we are actually reading a commentary by one world on the other. We are seeing what the "internal" world is saying about the external world.

The internal world differs from the external world in that the types of relationships existing in it are not boxed in terms of space and time. There is no space or time in this world. Instead, the relationships of the internal world are determined by aesthetic and emotional factors. Because of this, all travel or motion in the internal world occurs outside of the restrictions of time and space. Therefore, both time and space can be viewed and by being available to our vision, interpreted. In short, because of the nature of the internal world which is outside of time and undefined by it, time can be seen and, accordingly, read. Further, since there are no spatial dimensions and, therefore, no directionality to the inner world, travel is possible both forwards and backwards in time.

Now, I don't want to be accused of being a, uh, the term I have in mind won't be printed by my publisher, but let us say one who exaggerates to the point of losing track of the truth. I have discussed the limits of fortune-telling and time travel elsewhere and while I believe it is possible to "see" the future just like with our physical sight, I believe our psychic sight is limited. Just as I can't see Mount Mehru from my patio, I also rather doubt that I can see the third millennium from there either. But I do believe that we have some limited time vision available to us and that just as a newborn's eyes need to learn to focus and organize what they see of the external world, we simply need to train our psyches to see along the time dimension.

Let's go back to your notes, descriptions, and drawings from your scrying exercise. Pick out a creature that especially struck you. We want one that was moving, if possible. A stationary figure has meaning, but not for this aspect of our exercise.

How was the creature moving? In what direction on your scrying surface? From where to where? What objects did it pass and what objects did it start from and arrive at? Write down a list of the objects at the beginning, the end, and those passed in between in separate columns. Do any of these objects link up or are they associated with anything in your everyday life? Write down your associations and why. This is an anchor to your external life. If the object is located at the beginning of the creature's path, it will probably signify a thing or event that is either in the present or in the past. I don't mean to be equivocal on this, but your psyche is telling the story and will begin where it pleases. You have to answer according to your feeling tone (or intuition) whether this starting point is the past or present.

If the object is located at the end of the path of movement, it is, either the present or the future. Again, you must decide on an emotional or intuitive basis which point in time is involved. Needless to say, if the point at the end of the path is the present, all of the movements preceding it are the past. If it is the future, the present will be located at some point along the previous path. It is important to locate this point.

If the object you are drawn to is somewhere along the path, it is undoubtedly the present or the immediate past. It is possible that such a point could be the remote past if there is an exceptionally strong emotional charge to the event or object situated there, but it is very unlikely that it is a point in the future (although this is theoretically possible) since that is what we are attempting to reach as an end result of the path.

Once you have focused on an object and determined its point in time, follow the motion and go forward on the path of the creature's movement. What objects do you encounter? Are you especially drawn to any one of them? Why? Follow the same process you did with your first object. Determine its association and links with your external world. Fix it approximately in time. It will either be an extension of the present or at some point in the future.

Continue this process with all or at least most of the objects on your creature's path. Write this information down. When you have finished, this time, instead of waiting, quickly write a history of the events and objects in front of you. Make it chronological from past to future as you've uncovered them. Now put it aside, but unlike in our other exercises, don't forget it. Mull your history around in your head. Refine it. Does it relate to your life? Could it actually be an accurate reflection of the way things are going for you? Are there any surprises?

After a day or so of this, go back. Re-write your history as you would a report for a history class. Make it as factual as you can. Depending upon the point where the present was located on the path of the movement of your creature, you have a picture of a part of your future as your inner world sees it from outside of time. The next step is obviously to test your inner perceptions. This requires that you remember what you predicted. As these things happen, note them down. Try to estimate a percentage of "hits" that is, events or occurrences predicted by your exercise. At first, the percentage may be disappointing. But the chances of just one hit are long enough that you should be able to see that there is certainly something to all of this. As you use this technique, you will find that your inner world becomes more and more familiar with the external world and consequently, more and more accurate in its predictions.

Okay, you say, I can see the future, so what? Remember our overly utilized Stinkpot Turtle? Just as it rises over time from the muddy depths of the Juniata River, breaking the surface and exposing more and more of itself until it is landed in all of its odoriferous glory on the river bank, so too do the undetected or hidden problems—like those of our marketing director and his German counterpart—rise from the depths of our lives and expose themselves. Once they are out and fully exposed, it is too late to try to keep them from disrupting your life. But if they can be seen before this point, action can be taken to neutralize them or to divert their energies. You are ahead of the game!

Further, since you know ahead of its appearance what this thing will become, you can perform any and all of the exercises and operations described in this book before anyone else sees the problem. You are comfortable, confident, and ready.

This, of course, assumes that the creatures lurking beneath the surface are like or at least similar to all of the familiar land animals you've encountered before. This is a big assumption. I remember a documentary on, what else, PBS, about the Marianas Trench, the deepest point in the Pacific Ocean. The greatest fascination for me was the array of bizarre and alien creatures encountered on the way down.

These animals were unlike anything seen even in the more accessible depths of the ocean and totally alien to the inhabitants of dry land. They were luminous, primitive, and all teeth and jaws. It was truly like visiting another planet. The upshot of this for our discussion is that what is lurking under the surfaces of our lives may very well be absolutely foreign and ungraspable to us. We may, even with our scrying technique, which, in reality, is only a view from the surface downwards, fail to comprehend just what sort of monsters we are dealing with. And this Creature from the Black Lagoon will undoubtedly slither up onto our very own private—or worse, public—beach sometime in the near future. The techniques that we have described earlier for assessing vague and prickly problems will only work if we have something we can examine. It is imperative, therefore, that we get a good look at the monster in our Loch so that we can get some idea of how to handle it.

This involves bringing the thing to the surface on our own terms and in our own time frame. We may even want to land the thing, but that may bring it into plain view and we may not want to be seen hacking up a sea monster by our friends and co-workers. You would have to be prepared to answer the obvious question, "What is *that* doing here?" Perhaps you can answer, "It's not mine. It just washed up here. Disgusting, isn't it? Don't worry, I'll clean it up." If you can do that and get away with it, fine.

How do we get a sea monster to come to the surface? The same way we got the pleasure of encountering the Stinkpot Turtle—with bait. Now you can weight your hook and drop it to the bottom and wait for a bite, or you can use a lure and move it through the creature's habitat. Fly-fishing, where you work the line on the surface until the creature comes to the top and strikes, is even better.

Obviously here we are not fishing for trout, but for forces, or connections, of psychic contents so we must use an appropriate bait. Since what we are fishing for is a good look at or a definition of, our potential problem, we need something that will bring it up for us and keep it there. Something that will catch its interest and draw it out.

My son and I used to fish. In Central Ohio, the best you can do is bass. Generally having no luck with the elusive bass, one Saturday we went to the local sporting goods store and took out a video on bass fishing. One point especially struck me from that tape; bass are predators. They are, therefore, extremely territorial. They don't go after bait or a lure because they are hungry, as we mistakenly think. No, they strike because they are angry. The lure has gone through their territory. The bass wants to attack because it is protecting its space. The bass attacks because it is irritated.

We can use this same principle in angling for our hidden problem. What we want is to trouble the depths to invade the problem's territory and nudge and irritate it so that it will chase us to the surface and break the water. Then we can see just what we are dealing with.

We have a black shape moving under the surface. We are unfamiliar with its movements and we can't clearly make out its outline, but we need to learn about it. What do we do first? We do what we always do when we need to exert power over something—we ask questions. We know how to do this, but this time we are asking a special type of question. We don't consciously know what we are dealing with, but we are also not newborns so we do have a storehouse of experience about and an orientation to the world—both internal and external. We start by asking ourselves the basic question, and, in fact, this question is the background and assumed question in everything we do from this point on to try and catch our fish. The question is one of analogy, "What is it like?"

I say what is it like because we don't know what it is. However, since we all have a vast storehouse of life experiences, or, even if we have a limited amount of experience, we still have a series of mental cards which we can hold up next to our monster until we find one that matches something in it, and we progress from this one "hit." One "hit" is enough to start pulling a net around the creature.

Suppose you were shipwrecked in the Indian Ocean. You are on a tiny atoll off the shipping lanes. There are white beaches, coconut palms, and a deep blue lagoon in the center of the island. You are exploring and you are nervous since you have no idea what type of animals may inhabit such a place. Since you are alone, you could very well disappear down some beast's gullet and not a soul would know. Therefore, it is of paramount importance to you to find out what is sharing the island with you.

You tramp about the small island. You hear muffled noises in the brush. Maybe you see a quick movement in the shadows under the trees and vines. A bit freaked and tired, you drop to the pure sand on the beach and stretch out. You might want to swim. Or, better yet, fish. You peer into the tide pool. Something catches your eye. A dark figure is moving deep in the water. You now know you are not alone. What is it? What do you know about it? Nothing? Don't jump to conclusions in your fear. You know something about it. What color is it? You don't know, really. Well, what color does it appear to you? Black, big help. But it is a help. You know now that it has no internal luminescence of its own. It doesn't glow. It's moving. Okay. Does it seem to move under its own power in a "purposive" way? If it does, it is probably alive. It is not a machine or some phenomenon of the tide or the water current. Look closer, what shape is it? Is it round, or squarish, or elongated? It's elongated. Then it probably isn't a turtle or a crab or a crustacean. It also isn't a ray. It's in water, it's elongated. How long has it been down there? As long as you've been on the beach. It hasn't come up for air. It's a fish. But what type of fish?

Look again. Is it long and sleek or is it stubby? Long and sleek. Not a good sign. Is its head fairly large around the jaw area or does it taper to its jaws? The head is large and widens to the jaws. There is a very good chance, my friend, that there is a shark in your tide pool. And, if it is a shark, a salt-water fish, you know that there must be some underwater connection to the surrounding ocean. Not a great idea to go swimming in this pool. But you also know that sea animals, edible sea animals, have access to the pool. You now have some control over this part of your environment.

Let's look at this process again. There is a step here we don't want to miss.

When you were asking questions of the shape moving in your island pool, you were also performing another operation: comparing, as we said above. It was like you were pulling cards from your mental file drawers and placing them next to what you saw. Round shape, pull up a turtle, or a crab, or a clam. Does the shape look anything like these? No. Okay, discard them. Now we know something about what it is not. Elongated. Pull up the cards. All fish. Fish are basically elongated. Pull up the fish cards. Place them next to the image at the bottom of the pool. Is it stubby like a flounder? No. Like an angel fish? No. It's longer. We keep comparing fish length from our files until we find the cards of those fish that begin to match our shape in the pool. Where do we go from here? What else could we use to further distinguish fish? Head shapes. Does it get broader at the head? Does it taper to the jaws? It gets broader. Its face is almost all jaws. Discard the tapering headed fish. This sucker is a predator. Intuition closes the gap. Shark! We plunk down the shark card. Yup. It's a match. In our day-to-day life, it would be a definite advantage to know who and where the sharks are!

So we can learn something even about indistinct shapes by asking questions. However, we need to get a good look at our problems so we must push the process even further. We already have some experience with poetry and we are going to use three poetic tools to draw our problem to the surface. We are still asking questions (and exerting power) and we are still asking the basic question—"What is it like?"—but we are now using analogy, metaphors, and similes to change this question slightly and make it more specific. Now we are narrowing things by asking "Is it like. . . ?" Is it like a bird? Is it like my Aunt Sara? Is it like a bread box?

So that we are clear with our terms, an analogy is a situation in which if two things agree in some of their aspects, they will probably agree in others. For example, if I want you to build something for me, but you are concerned that I may not have enough money to cover your expenses and fees, you may ask me to let a mutual friend hold an amount of money to show my good faith and to make sure that your expenses at least will be covered even if I eventually call off the job. What is this like? It is like a surety bond. It assures that I am acting in good faith and will pay you. What should our mutual friend do if I pull the plug on the job halfway through when you have already bought all of your materials? Why, give you the money he is holding. What he has is similar to, or analogous to, a surety bond.

Another example from religion. We cannot know the nature of God. However, from the Bible we know that God sometimes acts as if he were a father. Therefore, while we can't know God himself (or herself), since we do have experience of human fathers, we can get some idea of what God is like by comparing him to the human father we do know.

A metaphor is a phrase or word denoting a specific object or thing, but used in the place of another to suggest or show a likeness between them. The dictionary I used gave the example of "Drowning in money." I don't particularly like that example. Perhaps a better one would be the ebb and flow of civilizations. We say that a nation can be at high tide, or alternately have its fortunes ebb. We all know what this means but we also and at the same time realize that a nation is not literally a body of water. The ebb and flow of the sea is a metaphor for national fortunes. What is it like? It is like the ocean.

Finally, a simile literally compares two distinct things by

saying that they are like each other. "Cheeks like roses." "Teeth like pearls." The word "like" draws attention to the similarities between the objects. What is it like? It is like a rose or it is like a set of pearls.

This is not English 101, and, quite frankly, I get confused by these terms myself. The point, however, is that we often use these techniques to get a handle on things we don't understand or to describe things in a way that can be pictured—just like poets and artists. How did the Steelers play? They were like a steamroller! How did your daughter dance at the recital? She was light as a cloud. The basic routine, therefore, is, what is it like? It's like a. . .

An example of how this analogy can be useful comes again from the workplace. Most of us are familiar with the term "barracuda." We have worked with people of whom we've said, "Oh, Jane? Yeah, she's a real barracuda."

Remember the woman I knew who worked for a social service agency? How the agency went from actually helping people to being strangled with paperwork? This was the doing of a barracuda. What was she like? She was a barracuda.

But knowing a person is a barracuda, being able to characterize your problem as something, gives you power over it. You may not know how this particular person will act specifically, but you do have some idea how barracudas act in general or you wouldn't have applied the term. This label gives you some predictive powers.

Knowing this person is a barracuda, you can then ask yourself, "How do I protect myself from a barracuda?" Barracudas, you know, are highly fixated predators. Their ability to lock on to a target to the exclusion of all others is the secret of their success as a species. But is also a weakness. Since a barracuda can't lock onto more than one target at a time, how do you handle a barracuda? By giving it a target other than yourself! If it has its mouth filled with somebody else's entrails, it doesn't have room for yours!

A further problem comes, however, when the lagoon

starts to get empty. There just aren't that many groupers left and your odds are not as good as they were. The positive point is, however, that neither are the barracuda's. A barracuda is an eating machine. If there is food available, it just cannot help but eat. That is what happened to my friend's barracuda. She began eating division after division. Spreading, but never really assimilating her power base in the agency. Had she been something else, a sea snake perhaps, she would have napped for a month after swallowing her prey whole. It would have thus been thoroughly digested before moving on to the next meal. Barracudas don't act like that. Her neglect of the divisions she chewed up as she looked for other prey led inevitably to a breakdown in services and mounting complaints until the agency director (who was the male version of the barracuda—a bastard), found himself in front of a mob of angry consumers, and, in the lagoon alone with a still-hungry barracuda. That's right, the barracuda, oblivious to the complaints and insurrections around her, had one last target—the director himself. Of course he did the gentlemanly thing and threw the barracuda to the mob for a fish fry.

What's she like? She's a barracuda. How do you protect yourself from a barracuda? Any barracuda? A strategy is available once you understand what you are dealing with. First give it another target. Second, stay out of the way and let it feed until it explodes. Third, never ever fight it head-on or attract its attention. You see, poetics do have their uses.

Let's go back to our hidden or submerged problem. To approach it, we are going to do a variation of the scrying exercise we did earlier in the chapter.

Again, go to a quiet place. It doesn't matter this time whether it is day or night, and the lighting is not as important. Wear something comfortable, but not the exotic attire you wore for your previous scrying. Get into *seiza*, but this time hold your spine straight and your head in line with your spine. Let your breathing slow. The gentle ebb and flow of your breath is like the waves rolling upon the white, pure beach we saw earlier. The sand is like tiny, smooth, white pearls. The sun makes them glow in soft pastels. In the center of the sand is a round pool. It is a tidal pool and is like a deep blue topaz. It is as still as the crown of a blue stone and you can lean forward to gaze into it. The blue color is relaxing. You are at peace. This is truly an island paradise. Something that you may have dreamed about.

The water moves somewhere in the corner of your eye. You turn your head to see the movement. Which way do you turn? Where in the circle of the pool is the movement located? You see it again. Your mind is focused on the area in the pool where you see the movement. Look closer. What do you see? Describe it to yourself. Its shape. Its color. The way it moves. Do the best you can. Are you accurate? Watch it for a few moments. Can you see more? Do you know more about it? Do this as long as you need to until you reach the point where it is not giving you any more information. Now you must fish. You have a ball of fine, translucent fishing line with you. Unravel it. Now you are going to put a fly at the end. Keep the thing in the water in your peripheral vision. Don't lose sight of it, but don't look directly at it either. You must concentrate on attaching your fly. Look at the fly while you are keeping the thing in water in your sight. What does the fly look like? What is it like? Simultaneously looking at the thing in the water and the fly makes your vision blurry. Your sight is unfocused. Focus your sight so that by doing this you make the two objects overlap in your vision. Do they fit each other? If they don't at all, you need another fly. More than likely they will fit or be the same in some ways and different in others. Where do they fit? What part of the fly is similar to what part of the thing in the water? How are they similar? Color? Shape? Describe this similarity and put it in words. "The sea creature is like this fly because. . . " They are both red. They are both fuzzy. They both have teeth. They both wiggle when they move.

Since the sea creature and the fly are not exactly the same, try to find another fly in your kit that is a closer fit than the first. If you can find one, again, tell yourself why and how they are similar. I have been giving physical examples—shape, color, movement. Don't limit yourself to these when you ask yourself whether your fly and your creature are similar. If your intuition flashes a "yes," then take anything that follows as your key. As always, don't be critical. "These two things are similar because. . . " Whatever your irrational functions give you, save it and use it.

Keep switching flies until you have one as nearly related to the thing under the water as you can find in your kit. Now, attach it to the line and throw it out into the water. The real test of your fly is whether anything will come to the surface to get it.

The fly is floating on the surface. Out somewhere in the pool. Jerk the line slightly. You need movement to irritate and attract the predator. If you try this for a while and you get no response and you feel like you will get no response, pull in the line and try some other fly. If you have nothing left in your kit, take the information and ideas you have gotten so far from your comparison and make a new fly using those parts and anything you feel that you want to add. Cast it out and try again. Jiggle it. Make it look real. Like a real, tasty piece of bait, wiggling through the creature's territory.

When it is ready, the creature will strike. You have irritated it. You have invaded its territory. Its sleek muscles contract and then propel it like a rocket from the bottom of the pool. Jaws open, it snatches the fly as it breaks the surface. Its momentum carries it up out of the water. It's happening so fast! But you can still see it!

The Creature from the Black Lagoon is now briefly suspended above the surface of the pool. Take a good but quick look. Take in as much as you can. This is not simply observation. Try to take a mental snapshot of this being that has been cruising around under the surface of your life. Hold the picture in your mind. The thing itself has fallen back into the water and is gone.

Hold your snapshot in your mind's eye. Examine it. Get the details as clear as you can. Of course you won't have everything distinctly since this is an "action" shot and things tend to blur with motion. But do your best to make things out.

What does the creature look like? Is it a fish? Is it a dolphin? A whale? A serpent? A lizard? Is it some sort of plant? Only you know. What does it look like?

Write down a description of your creature. Describe its shape. How was it moving? Fast? Slow? Was the spine bending? Did it even have a spine? Color is very important. What color or colors was it? Describe them. Was it angry? Happy? Hungry? Did it show any emotion? If so, how? Its eyes? Its jaws and mouth? Write this all down.

When you have as accurate and satisfying a description of your creature as possible, it is time to turn to yourself. Things just don't "happen" to you, which is how we all like to feel when something we tell ourselves is "unexpected" occurs. We are simply passive victims, we tell ourselves. How could we possibly have had any part in bringing about the disaster currently running rampant through our lives? The simple fact is that every event, everything that happens to you is connected to you in some way, or it would happen to someone else. You are the focus for the events that happen to you and this means that you or some part of you are connected to them. You are drawing them into yourself. Others may help, but you have somehow put out a line to these particular events.

So we must focus on you, too. Hold your snapshot of your own private Nessie in your mind. Examine it again. Look at it closely. Imagine you are looking at the picture through a magnifying glass. As you are doing this, how do you feel? In other words, as you encounter this creature that has been lurking about, hidden from your view, but quite obviously having an effect on you, setting events and forces in motion, how does your discovery make you feel? What type of reactions is it getting from you? Note all of these. Note especially what about this creature makes you feel a certain way. Are you sad? Angry? Afraid? What part of the creature makes you feel this way? Is it its color? Motion? Its jaws? Write your reactions down. Naturally, don't censor anything. Note along with your reactions just what it is about the thing that makes you feel this way. Write as much or as little as you like.

You might at this point also want to use our time-scrying technique to get some feel for what time frame this creature is acting from in your life. At what point in the pool did this creature emerge? Where did he or she disappear again? Which way was he or she moving? Were either of these points the present? Or were they in the past? Close your eyes. See the pool. Hold it. Let your intuition flash. Now! Okay, locate the present. How much time do you have? Answer quickly. Don't "think." Don't censor. How much time? When will this creature emerge naturally in your life? And knowing that, how does this make you feel? Afraid? Anxious? Or does it calm you to know when and, at least, partially, what you are dealing with? Write these feelings down along with your time frame.

Go back to your feelings. Hold them and roll them around in your mind for a moment. After you've done that can you tell why you feel the way you do? Is there some reason or reasons that this image makes you feel like you do? Jot them down. Don't censor.

We are now ready to anchor these feelings and associations to the shore of the pool—to your life. You have just written down the reasons why you feel the way you feel after encountering your creature. Perhaps some of these reasons already connect to parts of your everyday life. If they do, then examine them and add more detail if you can. How do these feelings attach to your everyday life? Where do they connect? If you know where, I can assume that you already know or at least recognize what is happening. This creature from under the surface has led you to the underground stream of events in your life. You can see where things are going. Tell yourself what is happening under the surface of your life. Tell yourself what will happen if you don't alter the stream now. Write this all out for yourself and then read it. Seeing it on paper makes it real. These are words of power. You have seen the future of your own life. You are in a better position with this knowledge. Close your eyes. Place your feet flat on the floor, sit with spine and head erect and feel the power bubbling up through the earth and into the cavities in the soles of your feet. Feel the power pumping into your lungs. It is metallic green and glowing. Green heat. Let your vision fill every nerve and meridian of your body. Keep it in and let it circulate naturally.

Let your breathing slow. Relax and concentrate the power into a green ball at your solar plexus. Hold it there for a moment, then let it gently sink into your abdomen. Let it cool slightly and let it condense as it spreads vapors through your body. You are cool and in control of your own future. You know this for a fact. Perhaps, however, the reasons you gave yourself for your feelings did not include any overt connection to your everyday life. Without these connections, this exercise can have no meaning or be of any help to you. We must, therefore, uncover the underlying stream in your life that your creature inhabits.

Fortunately, as we know from your work on the nebulous problems of chapter 3, there are ways we can make sense of the apparently senseless.

Since we have an image in mind here already, we can begin from that. Draw your creature as it crashes through the surface. I would say to use color, and you should if that is how you perceive your creature, but sometimes our problems are gray little things that work their way into our lives

125

unnoticed for their drabness. Therefore, you can use anything from the most garish of colors to stark black and white. Be sure, however, to get as many details as you can. The more details there are, as we've seen, the more easily you can grab onto something.

Study your drawing. Now, once again, check your feelings. How do you feel about your drawing? What aspects of it make you feel this way? In black ink, note your feelings next to the areas of the drawing that make you feel a certain way.

Again, study the drawing and your feelings as noted down. Are you getting any associated pictures from your intuition? These would be very helpful. So if pictures do flash into your mind, sketch them quickly and without questioning them. When you have done this, try to relate them to your picture of your creature. You can place your creature in the center of your floor and place your intuitive drawings around it so that physically they are next to those aspects of the creature to which they are related. If you don't have any intuitive flashes, don't worry. Intuition cannot be forced and if it does not flash for you, you are being told by its silence that you already have enough information from your feelings.

You've noted down your feelings and arranged your intuitive sketches around your creature drawing. Now, go over everything and then try to give reasons why you feel the particular way that you do. Make specific connections to specific feelings. If there are now connections with your everyday life, then explore them as we've done above. If there are not, then we have to initiate contact with our intuitive function.

To do this, choose one of your statements of feeling and the aspect of your creature it is associated with. Get it loosely in your mind. What I mean by "loosely" is to read it over and then quickly switch your mind to your daily life. What do you see? Don't criticize. Don't censor. And don't think that whatever is shown to you is trivial. Your intuition never

126

deals in trivialities. Remember that your intuitive function, just like any of the other psychic functions, is primarily a survival mechanism. Survival is the most important need of any organism. Take whatever image flashed into your mind and record it. Either sketch it or describe it. Include everything. Now you have made a connection with your everyday life. What does it mean to you? Can you see the problem or the underground current running through your life but previously hidden? If you can't, then you can proceed in one of two ways. You can simply put this material away and stew about it for a couple of days and then return. If it is still unclear to you, add another layer of feeling and intuition. See if you have any other associations or pictures of this material. If not, you may want to wait a few days and then start from scratch again. I doubt, however, that you will have to do that.

On the other hand, you can take your materials and treat them as the mass of twisted entrails that we chopped up and read in chapter 3. The important point to remember here is that unlike the physical and obvious problems of chapter 3, the problems we are now dealing with are hidden. Through the techniques of this chapter we were able to give them visible form. We caught them and, as such we can handle them like the visible problems of the previous chapters.

It is one thing, of course, to comprehend or grasp a problem. It is, as we have been at pains to state, quite another to act upon it. In our exercises with Zen *koan*s and with the intuitive function, we have stated that the action appropriate to a problem that we have grasped is given to us as a flash of insight from our intuition. We must then simply act as the picture from our psyche has shown us how to do.

In chapter 5 we will explore further how to get even deeper into the forces active in our problems and how to eradicate the roots of these problems. This will also include a discussion of intuitive action and how to act radically.

CHAPTER FIVE

Take a Flying Leap

I have a friend named Larry, who I have discussed in my previous book *Professional Budo*. Larry is a particularly aggressive, but also relatively honorable, defense attorney. Larry and I have crossed swords on more than one occasion and we have both lived to tell about it.

A particularly nasty trial that Larry and I did together involved a drug shoot-out in one of the housing projects on Dayton's West Side. Four young men—from Junior Achievement, no doubt—had a marketing dispute and settled it by shooting up a residential area where children played and one ill-starred individual, our victim, had his internal organs rearranged by a stray nine-millimeter slug. Of course, none of the young entrepreneurs involved in the shoot-out would have ever intended to drill an innocent bystander. They were simply absorbed in wasting each other.

Nonetheless, Larry's client was arrested since a witness, that is, his best friend, put the only nine-millimeter gun involved in the shooting in his hand. The police had taken a nice videotape of the friend's statement in the local emergency room complete with the always flattering hospital gown. Seems the friend had been shot through the foot—which would explain why he was still at the scene and available to the police to do his civic duty.

About a week before trial Larry showed up at my office and dropped a shiny bullet on my desk. It was Larry's argument that his client had merely been acting in self-defense and that he, the defense attorney, had been contacted by our state's witness, the friend of videotape fame, who now completely corroborated Larry's client's story of self-defense. And, as the the friend had provided Larry (not the proper authorities, of course) with a slug that was now lying on my desk and which the Friend, our witness, now claimed had hit him also on the night in question and, God is great, had worked its way out of his leg that very morning! Larry demanded that I have this bullet tested at state expense to show that it came from one of the other guns in the said affray. In my usual calm and unruffled manner, I inquired into the state of Larry's mental health. A polite and very professional screamfest and name-calling session ensued and we found ourselves in the trial judge's chambers on a Friday afternoon (insult of insults—no lawyers ever work on Friday afternoon, including judges, so our guy was none too pleased to see us). The trial was less than a week away. Larry moved the court to have the bullet analyzed at state expense. I argued that this motion was untimely presented under the Criminal Rules, which have about as much bearing in a real criminal case as the fact that there was a full moon that night, and, I also pointed to the suspicious nature of Larry's acquisition of this piece of potential—I hate even to say it now—evidence. We now had a three-way screamfest in the judge's chambers. All very dignified, I assure you. Read the official record.

After forty-five minutes of this mind-shredding, my own brain—my second favorite organ as Woody Allen says—was jelly. There was a great void. Celestial music tinkled in the hollow of my skull. A solar wind blew luminous flakes of space dust. The Buddha in his guise as Maitreya, Lord of the Future, appeared on the moon disc and glided forward in my mind's eye. He smiled and raised his hands. I instinctively knew that in the next moment he would graciously tell me the meaning of life and my unique place in the universe. At that moment, however, an eighteen-wheeler of a thought slammed into my head squashing the Buddha and all of his accoutrements like a bug. Without thinking, my mouth opened and out came:

"Okay, damn it! I'll have this vorslunger thing analyzed if Larry's client's friend is declared a court's witness!"

For those of you who are non-lawyers and probably for most of you who are, the Rules of Criminal Procedure in Ohio permit either party or the court itself to move and have a witness declared a witness of the court. This means that both parties can cross-examine this bozo and cross is much, much nastier and looser than the direct examination I would have had to use if the friend were my witness.

Neither Larry nor the judge knew what to say. This rule was as arcane as some of the formulas of the medieval alchemists. Nobody but me and the summer law clerk who turned it up in an obscure research project for our office and put it in a memo that I actually read for once knew about it. Larry sputtered. The judge looked up the rule. By God! I was right, his Honor exclaimed, and, then with an evil Friday-afternoon-not-on-the-golf-course grin, declared the friend of Larry's client—a court's witness.

Now this afterthought, which I freely admit only occurred because Larry had so irritated me that afternoon that I was just groping for something to tick him off, proved itself invaluable at trial.

The Rules of Evidence are a thorny path for the prosecution. We must actually present a case. The defense attorney could go out drinking the night before, show up hungover, and spend his or her entire time taking ill-natured pot-shots at our case and still be thought to have done a good job. If the friend had been our witness, he could have admitted that he gave a statement. He could have agreed to the substance of it. Then, on cross, by Larry, he could have said that the police beat it out of him. That it was all coerced, etc. Under these circumstances, I could not have actually played the tape since this was a witness not the accused and therefore his statement was not a confession. Further, I couldn't cross-examine my own witness. Therefore, he could say all sorts of untrue things and I couldn't challenge them. I could try to have him declared a hostile witness, but that would be rolling the dice in front of the jury and, I would have to show surprise which I could not do in this case.

But with the friend as a court's witness, I could ream this guy an extra bodily orifice and let the birds fly through on their way to Capistrano.

I showed the friend and the jury his videotaped statement putting the nine-millimeter gun in Larry's client's hand. I asked if this was his statement. Yes. Did Larry's client have the nine millimeter? "I didn't say that."

Okay. We ran the tape for everyone again. All told I ran the tape four times. I got it accepted into evidence. It went back with the jury during deliberations. They convicted Larry's guy after three hours.

When I went back to talk to the jury after the trial, they all stated that every time they had any doubts—and it was a confusing case—they just played the videotaped statement. They convicted on the basis of that statement. Having Larry's client's friend declared a court's witness—a spur of the moment thing, never really a part of my trial strategy—was a stroke of unmitigated genius. And this is precisely how the intuition works.

We briefly discussed the intuitive function of our psyches in chapter 3. To recap, we stated that both our feelings and our intuition comprise the two irrational functions of our overall organism. Feelings we said were constant. They attach to a thing or a situation and endure as long or even longer than the thing or situation itself. Intuition on the other hand was seen to "flash" like a stroke of lightning. It comes without warning; "out of nowhere." Intuition is also distinguished from the feelings by being "visual" or rather, "pictorial." It speaks to us by showing us a picture. The picture is the solution. It is our blueprint for action and in its most charged state, it forces us to act and to act immediately. A highly charged intuition short circuits all of the other functions. And it should.

Since this is not a book that is concerned with the "rational" functions, thinking and sensation, we don't have to waste our time with "planned" or "well-thought-out" actions. The irrational functions do all of their "planning" *sub-lunae*. That is, we never actually perceive the process by which these activities are put together. We only see the finished product, in this case, the intuitive picture.

You might be asking yourself by now if acting uncritically on a sudden picture that happens to pop into your mind is a very reliable way to approach things. Being the quasi-Jungian that I am, and, believing that the healthy adaptation of the human organism depends upon balance, specifically the balanced use and expression of all four of our psychic functions, I can definitely answer: Not always. No function is to be devalued. However, since what we are discussing in these pages are precisely those problems that have no rational solution, we are left with no choice but to try something else. If we have not developed our irrational functions, then we are in deep, deep do-do when our rational functions fail us.

And how does a person develop his or her irrational functions? By use, of course. Trial and error. The very way that we learn anything and everything about our world. We have to learn to trust our own irrationality. I use the term "our own" irrationality since the irrational functions we are using belong to us. They are us. Individually. Uniquely. It is my irrationality that I invoke in my world. It is your unique and personal irrationality that you invoke in yours. What we have been doing all along in this book is to learn to call, and once summoned, use and trust our irrational functions. Hopefully by this point we have seen that they can and do speak to us and, that they can provide creative advice and solutions to real, perhaps the most "real," problems in our own real worlds.

While feelings are, as we have seen, reliable guides with which to approach our problems, both feelings and, on the rational side, sensations, are more reactive than active in nature. They respond and report on stimuli, they don't actually approach or confront these stimuli presented to them. Feelings and sensations do not change an object. They add to it.

Intuition, on the other hand, very much like thinking, its rational brother, goes out and meets the object head-on and offers us ways to "move" or change the object presented. Both intuition and thinking grab the object. They are active functions.

Again, I am not saying that one aspect of our psychic functions is to be preferred to another. Reactive functions may very well be the preferred response to a given stimuli in a situation where action could get you killed. You see the cobra on your path. You freeze! You don't try to grab the snake or kick it. Aggressive action in such in instance would lead only to the annihilation of the organism, i.e., you.

There are, however, situations, and these are the type of situations that we have been discussing, in which action and swift action must be taken. Such action calls for irrationality and the active irrational function of our organism is our intuition.

So far we have learned how to approach and "read" situations using our irrational functions. We have encouraged our feelings to speak to us and we have invoked the pictures of our intuition as commentary on our more difficult problems. Now we need to learn how to charge our intuition in such a way as to incite, no, not incite, but to boot, big army boot, us into action.

As part of the research for my previous book, I read a short Japanese treatise called the *Hagakure*. The *Hagakure* was written by a retired samurai-turned-monk named Jocho Yamimoto. It was perhaps the most irrational book I have ever read. It was also, once one understood its context and who it was written for, one of the most insightful books I have ever read.

Jocho was writing a book of instructions on martial philosophy, on how to live as a samurai. The cornerstone of his view and advice was that the way of the samurai is death. He followed this with the corollary; when facing a situation in which death is just as likely as life, always choose death. This was the sum and substance of his advice to prospective warriors.

How insane, I thought. However, when it was remembered that the profession of the warrior, the samurai, is war, then the reality is that death is an ever-present fact. It is the extra comrade seated by the camp fire. If you fear death as a samurai, you are in the wrong profession. If you understand and embrace death, then you can carry on to perform your tasks to the best of your ability, and, concentrate on making them works of art in themselves.

What am I babbling about, you might ask? The samurai's profession is conflict. Conflict occurs when two or more antagonistic powers are vying for the same space. This is the essence of all problems. It can even be written mathematically, $1+(-1)=1$. This is, of course, absurd in pure mathematics. This is because mathematics has been appropriated by the thinking function. It, $1+(-1)=1$ makes perfect sense to the irrational intuitive function. Add one antagonistic element to another and only one can survive. That is the essence of all conflict. Conflict is a problem.

We have all heard about Freud's "fight or flight" concept of the survival instinct. When faced by the jaguar in the woods, there are only two choices left: fight or run like hell! All problems, at least all problems that are of practical as opposed to merely academic interest, involve only these two choices and a choice must be made.

I have a friend who is a colonel in Army Intelligence. The first thing that every prospective officer learns in Officer Candidate School, he tells me, is "Lieutenant, make a decision." Any decision. In combat, sitting around will more likely than not get everyone killed. Make a decision, Lieutenant.

Fear is the biggest enemy of decision-making and action. Why? I put it to you that it is not because we fear to get hurt, but rather, and this is the unique legacy of Western Civilization, the fear of making the wrong decision. This fear, I also submit, is illusory. We only can possibly know that a decision is wrong after the fact. Twenty-twenty hindsight, as we've often heard.

Jocho had something to say on this point also. He asserted that because we are all finite human beings facing death, we can never know the final outcome of our actions. Because of this Jocho, claims that there is no such thing as a just war. Never fight because you believe in the justness of your cause since history and future generations will continually re-evaluate all of your actions.

When I was growing up, John Wayne was a big hero to us all. We saw him fighting the Indians. Clearing the frontier so that nice white folks from the East could turn everything into farm land and towns. We cheered. We thought it was great. Ten years later, this was not the prevailing view. How dare we pernicious white folk destroy a viable and valuable alternative culture every bit as complex and productive as our own! Why, Big John was stealing this land from its rightful owners. Now, thirty years later, we are in the middle of a conservative groundswell. Ol' John may be rehabilitated. Who knows? Jocho knows. We can never know the final outcome of our actions, nor can we believe or be motivated to action by the apparent rightness or wrongness of these actions. When faced with a situation in which death is just as likely as life, always choose death. Fight like a fanatic, Jocho advises, and you may fail, but you will not act dishonorably.

There is also another fallacy to the "wrong decision" fixation. I call it the Fallacy of Finality. In other words, the world ends abruptly with the making of the "wrong" decision. A cosmic buzzer sounds and the game is over. Such a position neglects the fact that life and the world are infinitely complex, and, that the human being is also incredibly flexible. We will explore this more in the next chapter, but for now accept the fact that you, yourself, are such an infinity that you cannot even be defined. By being human, you are always and everywhere one step ahead of any definition of yourself. In other words, even in the most adverse of situations, you are capable of an infinite variety of actions and alternative adaptations. You move on.

What we must do then, after learning how to "read" a situation, is to learn to act. By acting, however, I don't mean what passes for action in most of our everyday lives. I don't mean simply doing the minimum to "get by" or, just letting events roll over us. I mean action that is obvious and unmistakable. I don't, however, mean action just for action's sake, so once again we must touch base with your real-life situation.

By this point we have done a lot of work together uncovering, describing, and responding to situations and problems in your life. You have amassed quite a pile of material, and I hope you have become more sensitive and aware of the connections and interactions of events, people, and things in your life. Now, just as an exercise at this point, we need to do something with this material. Later, we will expand our work into our lives.

Relax. Anywhere you want. It would almost be better for this exercise if you were a bit distracted. Take a piece of notebook paper and quickly jot down ten actual problems, uncomfortable situations or things that need to be resolved in your life right now. Don't think too much. Let your feelings and intuition give you the answers. They have been dying to do so, I can assure you! The size of the problem, intellectually at least, is of no consequence. The only criterion is that these situations must be currently active and working themselves out in your life.

When you have your list of ten problems or situations, don't read it. Cut the paper into ten identical strips and fold them so they can't be read. Throw them into a hat, shoe box, beer mug, trash can, whatever. Toss them so that they are completely mixed. Have another piece of paper handy. Pick one slip at random. Unfold it. Read the problem. In five seconds jot down an answer. By answer I mean a response that while not necessarily resolving the situation totally at least meets the situation and is a step in resolving it. You are used to this by now, but take the first word or, more importantly, pictures, that come to your mind. No criticism. Speed is of paramount importance here since we are utilizing and stimulating our intuitive function, the distinguishing feature of which is its lightning speed. Also since we are focusing on intuition exclusively here, I am not even interested in your feelings at this point. Place them gently to the side and proceed—quickly.

Pull every slip from your container and immediately write down a response. Take a breath. Look at the clouds. Listen to the birds sing. Go back to your answers. Compare them with the questions or problems. How do they appear to you? Are they really a lot of nonsense or is there something to your answers? Only you can do this, but I want you to look at the problems and answers again. This time, see if you find a situation that perhaps you had previously been mulling over and perhaps had began to come up with a "rational" solution for it. Write out your "rational" scenario for solving this problem. Are you really satisfied with this approach? You may be. However, you may still have doubts. Now, take your "irrational" response. Take the idea, picture, whatever that you so quickly jotted down and expand it.

Present it to yourself as a real course of action. Present it as "rationally" as you did your "rational" solution. I believe that you will find that it was only the manner of presentation, that is, the "rational" format of presentation, grammatical, etc., not the underlying ideas themselves, that gave your "rational" solution its appearance of reasonableness. After you have formatted your "irrational" ideas the same way as your "rational" solutions, you may be surprised to find that the instantaneous solution provided so quickly by your intuition is at least as plausible and workable in reality as your more "rational" solution. Probably it will be much better—both effective and personally satisfying. Try this a couple of more times just to build your confidence. As a safety measure, take notice of your feelings concerning both types of answers. Consult them. Which ones are more satisfying and appealing to your feelings and why? You can write these things down if you wish, but for this exercise it is not necessary. Also, present both sets of ideas to your thinking function. While we are trying to train and use our undervalued irrational functions in this book, we must not do so at the expense of our rational functions. They are also adaptive parts of our psyches and have equally valuable survival skills to contribute. Balance is the key and the goal.

After you have done all of this, it is time to experiment in reality. You have to trust and believe. I, sitting in my comfortable armchair, have the utmost confidence in you, be assured. Put aside your notes and keep only the slips of paper with your problems written on them. Arrange these ten problems from what you feel is the easiest to handle to the most difficult. Let the problems arrange themselves for you.

When you have your arrangement from easiest to hardest, take the slip with your easiest problem. Again match it with your intuitive solution. Read this solution over. Draw it out. Make it a real course of action. You have one day. Do it. Exactly as you've put it down. Do it. If you chicken out, you have one more day. Do it. Every time you chicken out, I'll give you one more day. Just do it. For real. In your life. Follow the lead of your intuition. We've picked your easiest, lowest stress problem so you won't be afraid. What we are interested in is two things. First, whether the intuitive solution worked. That is, is the problem gone or is it still lingering in your life? Also, are you still alive? Are people still talking to you? Do you have all of your limbs and entrails? See, that didn't hurt a bit.

Second, if the answers to my above questions are positive, I want you to get the feeling of trust in your intuition. It works. You don't just have my word for it now, you did it. You used it and you resolved a real live, actual problem in your life.

I want you to do this again. Same set of problems. Pick one. Your choice this time. For any reason you want. Do the same things you did to respond to your easiest problem. Again, one day. Of course I don't know how difficult this particular problem is, but the object is the same. Make it work; see it work, trust your intuition. This is simply another reinforcement.

Finally, I want you to take the hardest problem on your list. The one you absolutely dread. Respond to it like you did to the others. Notice, however, that I didn't say "face it." We've already discussed and dismissed that cowboy stuff in chapter 1. If you could just simply "face it," we wouldn't be sitting here now. Respond. Respond creatively. I know that you fear and loathe this problem, but you are resourceful. You are running on all four cylinders. You know how it feels to exert power and you know how it feels to put a problem behind you. You have nothing to lose.

Remember a few chapters back when I told you how I had worked in a loan collection department at a university? How I hated it? How I went to law school to get out of it? Do you also remember that I took seven weeks of back vacation time and went to Europe to sweat out the application process?

My trip to Europe was a solo venture. I took a huge orange knapsack and did London, Paris, Vienna, Venice (which I loved), Florence and Rome. I can honestly say that the only city that made me at all uncomfortable was Rome. I was traveling with my trusty copy of *Europe on Ten Dollars a Day*. At the end of the entry for each location, there was a list of the local criminal rackets. Sweden, for instance, had a sentence or two in this section. Most countries and cities had anywhere from a half page to a page. Rome, the Eternal City, had page after page after page of local rackets. It also had a distinctly sleazy feeling to it.

My train, a Super Rapido, arrived at the Termini, the main railroad station in Rome. I got off the train after traveling from Florence and stupidly set my pack on the sidewalk as I tried to get my bearings. I turned my back. When I turned around, my knapsack and all of my possessions on that side of the Atlantic were in the hands of a fat little Italian man in a porter's cap. He did not, however, work for the Italian railway system. We stared at each other. I'm going to quote our conversation. The man spoke English, but he did have an Italian accent. I am not making fun of this man's speech, so please don't be offended. I am not stupid enough to ever lightly poke fun at any ethnic group—especially Italians. Anyhow—

"You needa a room, right?"

"Uh, yes. But. . . "

He turned, my bag still firmly in his hand.

"You come-a with me."

"But—look, uh, where are we going?"

"We go to a Pension, okay?"

"But, I don't know. . . "

And then he turned to me and put the deepest of all philosophical questions that I have ever encountered to me, "Whatta you gotta to lose?"

Well, there was my life, my belongings, my boyish chastity. Okay, I'm exaggerating. But I was in a strange and reputedly rough city. I mean, all of my lire were stuffed into my socks. I didn't have any idea where this stranger was taking me. I had seen plenty of Humphrey Bogart movies—and I wasn't Humphrey Bogart. He led me through the North African section of Rome, the Arab area, and nothing is more scary to Americans than these highly civilized, law-abiding people of whom we know absolutely nothing and are exceedingly proud of our ignorance. In short, I was terrified. I had visions of being sold at a market somewhere in the Middle East. For a lousy price, at that. My fears loomed like angry Jinn in front of me.

Where this fellow actually took me was to an old office building converted into a pension. It was run by two little old women in black dresses and very severe shoes. The room I got was one of the nicer ones I had seen in Italy. It had a desk and, wonder of wonders, a shower down the hall. I was in American pig heaven. A shower! In Europe! Thank you, Jesus!

The place was convenient to public transportation and to all of the tourist sites in Rome. Every night I walked through the Arab district and ate in a couple of small restaurants that catered to working class Italians and the guest workers from North Africa. I ain't dead yet.

As an aside, I can't help telling this, when it came time to pay my room fees, I had forgotten that I still had my money in my socks. Embarrassed, I dug my money out in front of the old women who ran the place. I was ashamed, obviously insulting their city. Their faces were like stone and then, they both howled with laughter. Probably the best laugh they had had since Mussolini. One lady looked at me with tears streaming down her face, choking with amusement and said:

"Roma no good, eh?"

We all three laughed.

The point of all of this for you is, "Whatta you gotta to lose?" Words to live by.

If you've learned to swim, remember how you first learned in shallow water? Probably in the four-foot end of the pool where your feet could touch the bottom. You learned. You swam like a fish—in the four-foot end. Remember your fear of swimming in the deep end? Rationally speaking, of course, there is no difference physically between swimming in four feet of water and swimming in twenty-four feet of water or one hundred feet of water. The same skills and the same principles are involved. This is what I am trying to tell you now. You have already swam in the shallow end. You have used your intuition to solve at least two of the problems on your list of ten. The skills and advice that kept you afloat and kept you from drowning there, will keep you safe here. The water will hold you up. You can't sink.

I'm not really suggesting it here, but sometime I am going to design an exercise where you pick a situation in which you need to survive in one piece. Then I would ask you to write out at least ten absolutely wrong things you could do in that situation. The exercise would be to pick five of them and do them in the actual situation. My guess is that you would, unless we are talking about gambling debts or an IRS audit, still arrive home that evening with all of your limbs and entrails intact and sleep as well as you normally do and, wonder of wonders, still have this situation over and done with.

I have been a lawyer for fifteen years. I currently work as an appellate attorney for the Montgomery County, Ohio Prosecutor's Office. We often get fresh, green, newly licensed attorneys in our division as a first stop in their training process. They are usually just fine; competent, even arrogant until the time comes for their first oral argument to the three judges on our Court of Appeals. Panic sets in. My counsel to them is that no matter what they do, get tongue-tied, stutter, wet themselves, no matter what they do, the argument will be over in fifteen minutes. The judges may ask questions. They either know the answers already and just want the attorney to say them, or they honestly don't. Neither case is threatening. If they know the answers, you lose nothing by fumbling. If they don't, your answer is as good as any other. At any rate, even if you faint dead-away, someone will revive you and you will still go home that evening.

Take your most dreaded problem. Take your intuitive solution. Do your energizing exercises from chapter 2. Follow the suggestions of your intuition and do what it says in real life. Call me in the morning.

When you have done this, ask the same questions you asked after responding to the other problems. Did your intuitive approach work? If so, how? And how well? Count your arms, legs, toes, and fingers. Hug your entrails. Have you been hurt in any way by acting on your intuition? I will bet the ranch that you haven't, but only you can decide that. If you feel that you have been hurt somehow, how? And again, how seriously? Do you know why you were hurt? Was it the idea itself or the way you executed it? In other words, did you act with conviction, or did you hold back? Did you try to hedge your bets? Again, only you can answer these questions.

As I've said, my bet is that you have survived just fine and your dreaded problem is safely behind you. I am not denying the possibility, however, that you may have experienced some uneasiness or discomfort. If this is minimal, examine its source. If it is substantial and you feel that the intuitive advice itself was at fault, in all likelihood you need to go back and establish a better link with your intuition. Do this exercise again from the beginning. Work up from the easiest problem to the hardest using all ten problems as training steps.

I remember a story I once heard about Michael Jordan. I think my son, also a basketball player, is the source of this story. Jordan was cut from his junior high basketball team.

Not once, but twice, I believe. He apparently lacked the skills of the other players his own age. He did not stop there, however, but practiced every day; a routine that included shooting one thousand foul shots per day. The more he practiced, obviously, the more his skills improved and the more he could trust his skills in the infinite number of game situations in which he would find himself over the many years of his career. Do you honestly believe that psychic skills are any less responsive to use and practice than physical skills?

Once again, I am willing to bet that you were successful in this exercise and you know basically how to act on your intuition, that is, how to act decisively and passionately. Now let's have some fun and expand on this.

A basic question: Do you think the future is pre-determined? That is, do you think that time is in reality, a "thing"? Do you picture it, more importantly, as some sort of cosmic two-by-four laid across a ditch of chaos between some primordial "beginning" and some apocalyptic "end"? If you do, you must also believe two things: First, since time is a thing, like a block of wood, you can't alter it in any way since you yourself are simply one of many fixed splinters. Second, since time is always and already "there" and can never be altered, theoretically if you had the power to see into the future, you would unquestionably be able see events that will occur since nothing can be changed. Time is a thing.

There is a consequence to this notion and two corollaries. First, the consequence: You can't change anything in your future. You are powerless. First corollary: Any power you might have to actually "see" or read the future is useless since you can't change anything. You would, therefore, be Cassandra, who foresaw the Fall of Troy to the Greeks and warned her countrymen repeatedly but was unable to change their fate. She went mad. The second corollary is that you have been wasting your time with my book since either you can't change anything, or, the changes are already written into your "script" and you could not act otherwise. Either way you have no power and my whole approach is based on the fact that you do have enormous reserves of power.

But is time really a "thing"? We have been taught to see it as such. We hear about time being the "fourth dimension." When we conceive of this, we "see" something like a hyper two-by-four out there in the cosmos. After all, the other three dimensions are spatial, analogously, (aha! that word again!) time, also a dimension, must be just like the other three spatial dimensions.

Question, however: Are you able to "see" all of the space of the universe? Do you comprehend, do you know every piece or glob of matter contained in infinite space? When we think of our three dimensions, we think of a nice straight board. Three perfectly straight, Euclidian lines running perpendicularly to each other into the three perpendicular infinities. Did you know, however, that cosmologists have not pictured space like this since the last century? Would it shake you to know that space is seen as "curved"? It doesn't follow nice straight lines to infinity or anywhere else for that matter.

Which brings us to two more problems with the time-as-piece-of-lumber idea. First is infinity itself. Is it even possible for you to know any infinity? An example, name all of the fractions between one and two. I'll go put on a pot of tea. I'm whistling a happy tune. God! The Dayton Bombers are up two goals on the Cincinnati Cyclones! Oh, uh, do you have your answer yet? Of course not. It is impossible to know all of the elements of an infinity. So let's see, you can't know the shape of the universe, and, can have no idea what it is like anywhere except for a very narrow portion of it around your arbitrary blot of. . . of. . . what?

What? Which brings us to matter itself. The "stuff" of the universe. We have all seen, if only on children's cartoon shows, the equation $E=mc^2$. I'm not a physicist, but one of the implications of this is that matter is actually a bundle of

146

certain, abstractly and mathematically defined energies. It cannot be defined by what it is, only by what it does. Everything is action. Time, and the universe itself, is, therefore, not a piece of lumber. Not a "thing."

It could be argued that if we knew everything, we would see that all actions are determined and that time, once again, would be like a "thing." Ah yes, but, you, a finite being, cannot see everything. How, therefore, could you ever know this to be true? Further, since you can never know everything and since the universe itself is infinite, and active, how do you know that there is even any form existing anywhere except in the narrow region about yourself? How do you even know that the mental categories "time" and "space" apply in every part (I use the term very loosely) of the infinite universe?

One final point and I'll come back to planet Earth. You can't really define or accurately picture space and time. Do you think, however, that you can at least define yourself? Yeah? Okay, go ahead and tell me everything about yourself. You, too, of course, are composed of an infinity of action. Complete definition is therefore impossible. But even if you could tell me everything about yourself up to this moment, you have to realize that you the person who is telling me all of this is outside of what you are telling me. "And finally, I am telling you all of this about myself, including telling you that I'm telling you everything about myself," uh, but now that's changed because you've acted again, so, okay, "Now I'm telling you that I'm telling you that I've told you that I told you everything about myself," but, uh, I've, uh, acted again, so "I'm now telling you. . . " Sounds like a demented Monty Python routine, doesn't it? You ain't dead yet, is the point. "You," your personality, cannot fully be defined until then, the moment of death, because up until that point, you continue to act. To scare you, I'm going to drop the name Jean-Paul Sartre again. This existentialist philosopher argued, quite convincingly, that as a human being, we can never be defined. There is always, just by the nature of our existence as human beings, a part (again loosely used) of us that is always one step beyond what we "are." We are like worms borrowing through the ground. We pile up dirt behind us. This is our trail. Our lives, if you will. But while the pile is our life, we are not the pile itself or our "lives." We are the burrower. The one who acts. As long as we act we are not a "thing" and we are, just like any other infinity, indefinable.

At the beginning of this book I spoke about the Buddhist view that the universe is composed of things called *dharmas*, globs or blots of experiences, and "spaces" between them called, "unconditioned *dharmas*." We wanted to access these unconditioned areas because, being unconditioned, anything was possible there.

You may fairly object at this point that we did in chapter 4 precisely what we are now saying cannot be done. We read the future. Am I not, therefore, contradicting myself? No, I am not, and the reason again goes back to the nature of time itself. I said in this chapter that we should not view time as a "thing." To do so not only prevents any creativity in your life, but is also impossible to do because of the nature of the universe and of human beings. But is there any other way to look at time?

The answer is yes, of course. And the way that we look at time so as to be consistent with our lives and our universe is the way our intuition conceives of it. When Carl Jung defined the four psychic functions, he asserted that the intuition was the function that saw and presented possibilities. It takes the given and from it draws out the various strands and presents to the ego possible futures. Are these possible futures "real"? If they were not, we would have no intuitive function. We wouldn't need one. If time were a thing and the future already fully existed, what would be the use of a function that presents alternate futures? If alternate futures can be conceived, then this part of our minds must have access to something outside of the block of wood we call time. If there is something outside of time, then time itself either does not exist everywhere in the universe, or, there are other times possible, or, time is not a set thing. The bottom line in all of these scenarios is that alternate futures are possible.

Time-as-a-thing presents the image of a box. It confines life between set and fixed boundaries. It constricts and kills. Such a time, however, does not exist except in the necessarily limited world of physical science. Such an artificial time is a measuring device only. Real time, time that is lived by a living organism, is not a constricting thing like a trap or a jail, but a key that opens up three spatial dimensions to an infinity of possibilities. Time is the home and category of the possible. It makes space, it does not confine it.

This view is nothing new or unique to me. I stole it unashamedly from Martin Heidegger. The point is that in our scrying exercise, an exercise in which we looked at the flow of time and saw the future, we really were looking at time. At real time. Time as the cradle of possibilities. Due to the choices and judgments made by our intuition, we saw one possible future. That is not to say that there are not others. But your intuition drew one future for you as likely, given the information it had. It was a prediction, not a certainty, since time is not a category that deals in certainties. Because we are always dealing in infinities, and, are a type of infinity ourselves, no time—past, present, or future—is absolutely certain. If you believe that the past is set, go back and read the comments by the samurai Jocho Yamimoto. The past, like the future, is continually being rehashed and reinterpreted. It, like the future, is still alive, and, alive with possibilities which is the meaning of life.

Returning to Jocho, all that we have in our lives is our actions. The future is not set and the past is unreliable. This is not scary, it is wonderful! Creation would not be possible without this state of affairs. Therefore, seeing that we can act on our intuition and that the consequences of doing so are no worse than other, more "rational" courses of actions, and, seeing that the future is a garden of possibilities, of alternative paths, and then finally realizing that as a human being, that is, just because you are a human being, you cannot be defined and are not now defined, let us create a possible future.

Why would we want to do this? Because I want you to come to see your life as the raw material for a work of art. Your work of art. Many times we have heard pompous asses say "My life is my work of art." I guess I'm just one more. But the fact is that our lives are created by ourselves. While it is absolute nonsense to believe that we can create every aspect of our lives, it is also totally absurd to whimper that we have no control at all. We all have some control. There is no art without some control and there is also no art with total control.

As I've said, when I was in Italy, I went to Florence. The high point of my entire European trip was seeing Michelangelo's breathtaking statue of David. There is something uncanny, almost divine about the statues this artist created. I have heard other people say this, and I will confirm it also, you swear that you see these things breathing! At any rate, when I returned to New York, I did some reading on Michelangelo and found that the stone the artist used for this overwhelmingly magnificent monument was in fact a badly damaged and rejected hunk of marble that nobody particularly wanted. It had odd gouges in it that made it too hard to work with. Michelangelo chose this piece of marble and worked the imperfection into the overall effect of his David. Did he have complete and total control over his art? No. He did not create the marble he used. He did not create the ugly gouges in it. If he had had a choice, I am sure he would have chosen a more perfect piece. But this is the point, art is beautiful, not perfect. That is why it is art and not religion. Art is the joining of human freedom to the given. The possible joined to what is. Just like Michelangelo, there are givens in your life. You, however, can choose what possibilities to fuse with them. To that extent, you have some control. You are an artist.

Now let's create a future. We are going to write a story. Or, if you're more visual, we are going to draw a picture. I would tell you to go back to your slips of paper that had your ten problems on them, but that would be starting out completely negatively, and, we also already know what happened in these situations. Instead, jot down five or six statements describing your life situation right now. On another sheet of paper jot down seven to ten possible things that you really want to occur in your future. They can be as rosy, as overblown and outlandishly positive as you want. They just have to be at least, very thinly possible. In other words, flying under your own power is not terribly likely, but, the house on the lake might be. Spiritual enlightenment might be. Make these wishes possible but try to stretch possibility just as far as you can. This is fun. Fun is okay.

Take your starting points and your end points and write a story that uses them all. Make it so that you go from the points in your present life situation to the wish-fulfillment points in your future. Oh, by the way, this should be written like a romance novel. Schmaltzy, soupy, exciting, titillating. Live it up. If you claim that you are too, uh, macho for this sort of thing, okay, then write an adventure story (they are, after all, just the male version of romance novels). If you are more visual, illustrate all of this like a comic strip. Use some description, though. Remember, if while you do this, you are not laughing or getting aroused or at least thinking how silly it is—you are not doing your job. This is supposed to be silly. It is supposed to free you from the idea that your life is like a block of wood. Because that is a terrible analogy or metaphor or simile, a terrible and inaccurate way to see things. You still don't believe me?

Let's take a look at your "real" life and your romantic story. Both your "real" life and your romantic story start from the same point since I asked you when writing your romantic to start with five or so "real" statements about your "real" life situation. It is essential to remember that neither your "real" life nor your romantic story has occurred yet. There has been no movement as yet from your starting point. In fact, unlike your story, which you have created, you don't have any idea what will occur or, for that matter, what can occur in your "real" life. In that sense, as we sit here at this point in time, one story exists and one, the "real" life one, does not. No action has occurred concerning that "real" path.

In fairness, before devaluing the romantic path you created, you should at least have something to compare it to, not just some vague and unstated assumption about a non-existent but so-called "real" life. You've written your own romance or adventure about your future. Now, since you may view these as simply fantasy, write another story. Write down what you think will "really" happen starting from the same point. Make it as detailed as your other story. Write it in any style or in any way you want. Do "realistic" illustrations if you want.

Read through this new story. Depressing, isn't it? What does it remind you of? Do you remember anything you've read that is similar? Dickens? Victor Hugo (*Les Misérables*)? Camus? Maybe my particular favorite, Dostoyevsky? If it does remind you of another story, why?

You know what you've done, don't you? You've written just one more piece of fiction. The so-called "real" life you projected is fiction. It is no more "real" than your romance or adventure story. The difference between the two is only that of the literary style you've chosen to adopt. Someone, I think it was an ex-college girlfriend, an impeccable source, once said that we all tend to live our lives like we were reading about them in a novel or seeing them on the silver screen. Robert Klein, the comedian, used to do this routine about how to scare off muggers. When they begin to attack you, you treat them like they were in a movie by adding a sound track; you belt out the scary music from some horror film you've seen. This freaks them out since now they are in your movie. The point is, tritely enough, that it is your movie. Or your story, at least.

Oscar Wilde, in one of his essays, discusses how nature imitates art. He goes through an exercise where he compares such "natural" phenomena as sunsets and London fogs to paintings and literary descriptions. He points out how nature, never to be outdone, keeps herself abreast of the latest London and Parisian fashions and is seen each new season in what is fashionable for that season. The year before he was writing, Turner, with his orange bursts of sunlight, was the rage. Nature, not to be gauche, adopted Turner for all of her sunsets. People saw them everywhere. In the year Wilde was writing, Turner was passé. Nature this year was only to be seen in Renoirs and Monets.

Wilde's essay makes the essential, but rarely admitted point about our orientation to the "real" world. We see what we want or have been brainwashed into seeing. The future has not occurred and is only a repository of possibilities. No possibility outranks another. You can say one is more probable than another, but that is like saying that just because the ball has fallen into the black slots in the roulette wheel fifty times in a row, it must now fall into a red slot on the fifty-first spin. That flies in the face of all probability theory since there is no causal connection between the result of one spin of the wheel and another. When you assign probabilities to life, any life, yours included, you are literally pulling the numbers out of your, uh, ear. You are not a "thing." You cannot be defined. If you chose to assign numbers, you are engaging in a literary preference only. You are saying, "I prefer the style of Dickens to the style of Jackie Collins." Fine. But don't kid yourself into thinking that one style is any more "realistic" than another. They are both fiction.

Go back to your "realistic" account of what you think

153

will happen in your life. Take the important events out of this story and list them on a piece of paper. Leave some space between them. Next, for each, write a brief description of just how that event could occur. Remember, for one event to occur, it must be connected to all of the preceding events on your list which means that all of the pre-conditions for all of these preceding events must also occur. Care to assign probabilities to all of these events? If you are anal enough to do this, simply multiply all of your probabilities at the end and you will see in stark numbers just how likely—and unlikely—your "realistic" future is.

Go back; go through the same list of events. This time write down ways in which the key events you listed would not occur. Interestingly, you will find that the alteration of just one or two pre-conditions or sub-conditions of this chain of events will completely invalidate your "realistic" future. Assign probabilities to these couple of sub-conditions. Multiply them out. Your "realistic" future is not terribly likely, is it?

If you are some sort of Libran or Sagitarrian, you have an uncontrollable urge to be fair about all of this. Go ahead. You can't help yourself. Take your romance or adventure story and do the same process, assign probabilities to events. Multiply. Then think of ways these events couldn't happen. Assign probabilities. Multiply. Compare all of your results. It is a shameless truism, but because you are working in probabilities and because nothing in life is certain, you have to deal in probabilities, you can see that all of the futures you projected are only possible futures, and, I'll wager, at least the probabilities of either future not occurring are pretty damn close. Have you had enough yet?

The point of all this is that nothing is certain. Which brings us back again to our original discussion of the unconditioned *dharmas* of chapter 1 and in many ways the Buddhist view of life. I say Buddhist, and I can hear my mother-in-law, a devout Christian, giving me a hard time

because I'm a Buddhist and see the world this way. So I'll add
that while Western thought differs from Eastern, the practical outcomes, action over philosophy, is also a part of the Christian point of view. Both Christ and the Buddha when confronted by people who thought too much counseled them in no uncertain terms to stop wasting their time and pay attention to the one thing they did own and did have some control over—their actions.

That all aside, we stated that these "openings," these spaces between the dots of experience of our lives, were the spaces that allowed anything to be possible. They were not subject to "dependent arising," that is, they flowed from nothing and therefore nothing in them could be predetermined. Because of this we learned and practiced techniques that allowed us to enter into this space and its freedom. We claimed our energy and power and brought it there with us so that we could combine it with our freedom and use it as free men and women in the *dharmas* of our lives.

As aides to this process we made use of two parts of our beings that are usually devalued in our Western civilization and which are termed even in the sympathetic literature of Carl Jung, the irrational functions: feeling and intuition. Both of these functions were excellent guides and connections into and out of the unconditioned *dharmas* that we entered. They gave us added dimensions to our everyday life and therefore helped us more completely and accurately "read" the events, situations and problems of the conditioned parts of our existence. We also found that one particular function, intuition, because of its speed, impelled us to act. It, like its opposite rational function, thinking, is active by nature and has been developed by nature as a function that gives solutions.

Because our intuition gives solutions for future actions, we realized that if time were a completed "thing" and the future predetermined, there could be no intuition whose primary function is to take what is given by the world and present possible futures to us. We know, however, that we do have an intuitive function and time is not a "thing" but a mad pagan cornucopia of possibilities. This is all, of course, consistent with a world that includes the openings or holes we call unconditioned *dharmas*. These unconditioned *dharmas* make the space for all of these possibilities and thus, create time. They "make time."

Because nothing, no possible future is or can be certain, we have as with Christ, the Buddha, and, consistent with both, Jocho Yamimoto, only our actions. Since the future is uncertain, we must act only with and for the sake of acting. Since this is the case, we can act any way we want. We can act intuitively. As we experienced first hand in our exercises in this chapter, nothing at all precludes us from following the pictures our intuition flashes for us and making them real in the real world of our lives. Or, at least as real as any other "real" thing.

Acting this way is not new. There are two very good examples of this view of life and types of actions in the East. They are Zen *koan* practice and, the martial arts.

In *koan* practice, we learned earlier, the student is given a nonsense phrase or question that he or she must answer. The verbal answer is, of course, not itself important. What is important is the quality and energy content of the student. "Answering" one *koan* only leads to another and yet another until the student's brain is fried. The energy, *qi* or *ki*, builds up. This energy seeks release from this practice, eventually breaking down the barriers in the student's psyche and over-running the conventional and fixed energy channels which Jung calls "gradients" thereby energizing and bringing to life the whole person. Possibilities burst like firecrackers in a non-stop Fourth of July! The student is free. Unconditioned.

In the martial arts, at least in the Japanese forms, is a practice called *kata*. A *kata* is a set of combat movements, almost like dance steps, that the student repeats over and

over again. It is the martial form of the Zen *koan. Kata* practice—believe me on this one—also fries the brain. The
novice student thinks he is learning techniques that will help
him or her in a fight. In fact, that is not the object. The
object is to unlearn everything and act according to one's
intuition. Freely. Unconditioned by the opponent, who is, in
fact, oneself. Will it make you a better fighter? Why not.

In the next chapter, we are going to complete our discussion by again looking at the nature of the "real" world we
live in. By this point, since you are still reading me, and
assuming that you are not simply still reading because of the
American notion of giving me a fair trial before hanging me,
you have gotten some first-hand experience of a whole new
dimension to your world. You have developed and used new
power. You know you can act freely using these new energies
and frighteningly, you know now that literally "nothing" is
stopping you. What you may not know, however, is that this
"nothingness" comes directly from you and, you are therefore responsible for it just like anything else in your life.
Because, as you now know, you are free, you are also totally
responsible for everything, that is, you are responsible for
your actions. You can put the blame for your world and your
actions, therefore, on "nothing."

Accordingly, we are going to spend our final chapter
looking at "nothing."

CHAPTER SIX

"Nothing" Is Stopping You

When I was in high school I was stupid. I said stupid things. I thought stupid thoughts. And I made a virtual career out of dressing stupidly. But one of the dumbest things I did was to play football.

Now football is no dumber than anything else in life, contrary to public opinion. You chase an intrinsically worthless object around an artificially enclosed space with other people watching and your opponents just waiting to squash you like a bug whenever you get even remotely close to this useless but blindly sought-after thing. A good bit of all of our lives can be described in these terms.

For anyone who has not had the pleasure, football begins with summer practice. This occurs in the last two weeks of August. First, barbed wire is stretched around the dusty field (has to be dusty so that the dirt can coat your mouth guard), then the guard towers and machine guns are set up. Finally, the coaches are given their riding crops and monocles. The fun begins.

I weighed 138 pounds in my sophomore year and played varsity—the Hamburger Squad, so called because our only use to the team was to provide trampling material for the really good guys. Accordingly, I managed to have three—

159

count them, three—pairs of shoulder pads broken off my nmoback that season and one first-class varsity helmet cracked from my forehead to the base of my skull—in other words, split in two.

The season dragged on from August until November. We had a championship team so, joy of joys, we got to extend this inexpressively marvelous time into post-season play. When the season was over and I still had all of my limbs and entrails—others weren't so lucky—I heaved a sigh of relief, lit candles to the Virgin and vowed to join the Third Order of St. Francis. But football is a jealous mistress. My joy was short-lived. While summer practice was hell on earth, it had a younger sister called spring training. Summer practice was done in heat and dust. Spring training was done in cold rain and fog.

Our spring training sessions consisted of calisthenics (this was the sixties, they weren't known as aerobics yet), followed by weight training. All of us tender underclassmen thrown in with upper-class football players, wrestlers, Foreign Legionnaires, British seamen—well, anyone read "Billy Budd"?

After humiliating and exhausting torture at the weights, coupled with abject brutalization, we got to go outside in the aforementioned rain and fog to run the "short"—smile—cross-country course. This was a city school so imagine just how fast we ran in certain neighborhoods!

What I am now going to tell you deserves an award for epitomizing all that is stupid in stupidity. I am now talking real stupidity. When we had limped into the basement where the athletic department was located after the cross-country run—we boxed. We were Catholic adolescent boys, we couldn't have sex, so we turned to boxing as a socially acceptable substitute. Go figure.

Anyhow, we generally boxed the wrestlers who considered all football players to be basically ballerinas. We used eight-ounce gloves. Let me repeat this: We used eight-ounce gloves. For anyone in this civilized day and age who probably knows nothing of the old barbaric sport of boxing, eight-ounce gloves are basically big mittens. They are next only to bare knuckles (which by the way, got plenty of use in the alley behind the shoe factory a block away and out of sight of the nuns).

In those days I was incredibly stupid, as maybe I've said. I actually liked boxing. In fact, I was angry because our school, a Catholic school and therefore one of the last to do so, had stopped having a boxing team. Some nonsense about a kid having a brain hemorrhage.

But there was a pecking order here, too. The upper-class bruisers had it out first. We had to wait in line for our fair share of brain damage. A curious thing happened though. A friend of mine, a wrestler, also 138 pounds, kept beating the tar out of all of the bruisers, football players and wrestlers alike. We'd drag in from our run to be met by hulking monsters with blood running from their lips and noses, crawling from the boxing room. I watched a couple of bouts—three rounds, three minutes each—and saw that my friend, who was fast and mean and had had boxing lessons at the Y, never had a glove touch him. A tough, tough working-class kid.

One day as they rolled the corpses from the floor, my friend, Dane was his name, noticed me standing there, mouth open, gawking away. Having no one else to pummel, he called, "Hey, Katchmer, hey, George, c'mon, man!"

Now this reminds me of the old Marx Brothers routine: Chico and Harpo are broke.

Chico; "Oh, I needa some money! Right now I'd do anything for money. I'd kill for money! I'd kill you for money!"

Harpo's eyes widen. Chico warmly smiles and puts his arm around Harpo.

"Naw, you my friend. I kill you for free."

Well—here I was getting eight-ounce gloves tied on my hands and my good friend Dane preparing to alter my features, hopefully in a pleasing pattern, as Japanese Go-players

161

do to their desiccated foes.

My other good friends, my comrades from the football team, pushed me into the ring. Basically I tried to stay away from good ol' Dane, but in reality, spent most of my nine minutes getting beaten to a bloody pulp. All that was missing was steak sauce.

Then, in one of those epiphanies that God jokingly grants occasionally to lost souls, I looked up during a reign of blows to notice that ol' over-confident Dane had over-reached himself in his eagerness to finish me off. His fists and arms were about eighteen inches apart. There was, in short, a clear shot for his wide-open, until then untouched adolescent face. There was nothing stopping me (except, of course, fear of an even worse beating) and I had a pretty decent right. Yup. I hit him. Dane's head flew back. When his face snapped back, the world stopped. The look of surprise and shock on his face is something I warm myself with on cold evenings. And then, and then, and then—the blood started from his nose. I was a hero! The footballers cheered! The other wrestlers were suddenly close friends. Then, of course, Dane beat the living crap out of me and ground me into the floor—in a pleasing pattern—he was my friend, after all.

My moment of glory shares something with a lot of similar moments in everyone's lives and with life in general: There is a great deal of "nothing" in our lives and this nothing that makes such a large portion of existence is not a bad, depressing, or negative thing. It is an opportunity, an opening for creative action. The secret of life—you've heard it here first (if you don't count Jean-Paul Sartre, the Buddha and all of the existentialists, mystics and Zen practitioners throughout all of recorded history)—is that since the essence of life and existence is nothingness, nothing, literally, is stopping you.

But "nothing" is not quite as simple a concept as we all might think. Simplistically, if you have five hundred dollars and I take it, you have nothing. Or you may start with nothing. "What have you got?" Nothing. "What was that noise?" It was nothing. "Look!" There is nothing there. We all think we understand what "nothing" is.

Isn't that an interesting sentence, however. "We all think we know what nothing is!" Can "nothing" exist? This sentence implies that it can. What is there? Nothing is there. Am I just playing games? We all speak like this and we all understand what we mean when we say these sentences. But how can such a phrase—"nothing is"—make sense?

When we say the word "nothing," we tend to mean the absence of something or, more expansively, the absence of anything. There is a clever way to dodge the problem. Simply add a hyphen to the word to get "no-thing." Nothing then really is the absence of "things." Where have we heard this before?

Ah! Yes! We've heard this sort of speaking when we discussed time and, human beings. We said that only totally completed entities were "things." Things do not act. Or more accurately, they do not interact. They are self-contained. There is nothing beyond them. This is where we start getting existential. Sartre stated that things exist in-themselves. They are dead by definition and the only existence that they actually have is for us. We are human beings and therefore, we are non-things. Nothings. We are what "things" are not and can never be. According to Sartre, our entire nature is negative. We as humans are the beings who secrete nothingness into the world. How is this done?

What is the first thing that toddlers do when they finally become conscious of themselves as separate and distinct human beings? As separate existences? They say "no." Johnny, do you want Cheerios? No. Suzy, pick up your ball. No. Anyone who has had children knows that there is a stage when a child says "no" to anything and everything. It is how they become human. To say "no" is the essence of a human being. We as human beings bring negativity, nothingness,

163

into the world as our unique contribution.

Before you throw this book across the room as thoroughly depressing and not helpful at all, remember the corollary that is joined at the hip with negativity—freedom. Not a bad thing, eh? The nature of freedom is choice. It is the ability to say "no" to things as they are. We all, as human beings, have the ability and urge to say to "reality," "No, this won't do."

Where have we discussed freedom before? Why, in the context of creation. Art. We defined art as the joining of human freedom with the given. Ought with is, so to speak. And, haven't we heard these two terms, "creation" and "nothing" being used together somewhere else? God created the world from nothing! Not only is nothingness not, therefore, a negative and thoroughly depressing thing to be overcome and avoided, but there could be no existence at all without nothingness. Nothingness makes existence itself possible.

Possible? Wasn't the nature of time to be the repository of all possibilities? Stepping back to our dead German friend Martin Heidegger (and Søren Kierkegaard, for that matter) the nature of man is to exist in time; that is, in the possible. Existence is in time and is composed entirely of possibilities. A "thing" has no possibilities. Its only existence is the borrowed existence it gets in the possibilities given to it by us.

Since we are free and we have the power of negativity, we are creators, artists. A pretty positive thing if you ask me!

I think people picture Sartre as this froggy, little bug-eyed man sitting around some Paris café after the war, chain-smoking and drinking cup after cup of bitter coffee, being a depressing guy by profession. The popular picture of existentialism on this side of the Atlantic is black, dower and, well, negative. However, if God Himself uses negativity to create the world and a specific type of world at that—one of infinite possibilities—how can we say that this philosophy, or any philosophy—Buddhism comes to mind—derived from a starting point in nothingness and freedom, be considered anything but an absolute joy?

We have, as we discussed, one psychic function that deals exclusively in possibilities; the intuition. The intuition presents (note the time element) pictures of possibilities to us, since it sees clearly that what separates us and this moment from the future is nothing. What is stopping you from going back to school? Nothing. What is keeping you from working out? Nothing. Nothing stands between you and the future. You can respond that time does, but time is simply an infinity of possibilities. Time is not a thing. Nothing stands between you and the future.

This book is about problems. Sartre defined the human being as the being whose being is a problem for him or herself. Problems are, therefore, unavoidable for us as human beings. Again, depressing, huh? And again, no.

As I've said before, we have four psychic functions. One, the intuition, is the most in sync with the nature of existence. That is, with time and the possibilities that make us human. What function do you think is closest to the nature of a "thing"? A "thing" by definition is complete. Finished. Dead.

When we study something "scientifically," what do we do? The first thing we do is to draw arbitrary limits. We are studying x and nothing else. We can't have contamination from anything outside of x, or the experiment won't be valid. What if x is a human being? Why, then, uh, we will only study his or her observable external behavior. But behavior is so complicated. Well, er, then we'll only study x's response to a specific and limited stimulus, y. We have succeeded in making x, a human being, into a "thing." Complete and unvarying. That is the object of all law and all science.

The ally of law and science has always been logic. The trouble with logic, however, as shown by Russell and Wittgenstein, is that it is sterile. Dead. If you know one logical proposition, you know all other logical propositions that

165

can be derived from it. Logic is the clinking of "things" against each other in the world.

What are we talking about when we speak about science and law and logic? Why rationality, thinking, of course. Thinking, while useful, is as close to being a "thing" as a human function can come. This does not mean that thinking is bad, it simply means that it is only a very limited tool of the total organism. In the East, the mind is seen as just another sensory organ. It is complicated and organizes the other senses, but it can no more exist by itself than an eye-ball can.

The intuition is the most human of functions and by presenting the possible, it is the most negative. Intuition creates life. Intuition makes us free by showing us that nothing is stopping us.

In the last chapter we used this idea a bit when we drew up our romantic or adventure stories about our lives and contrasted them with the "realistic" story we wrote using the same starting point. We found that for practical purposes, the actual living of our lives, the futures that we created—and we created them all—were all pretty much equal in likelihood or, at least, equally liveable. They were possible; do-able.

Having done this, however, we still may be tempted to say that while we can live a number of possible futures, they still are basically limited by the personal "realities" of our lives, that is, our pasts. Of course, this is patently absurd since the past, like the future, has now slipped into the realm of possibilities. We can turn to look at it, but like the future, we now have the power to play with it, too, making of it what we will. If we use the term "reality" then the past is no more "real" than the future. They are both simply things to muse about by the fireplace with a glass of port and a hunk of cheese. We create them both.

In order to once again see this fact, and to actually experience it, we are going to "read" time. We are also going to examine just what sort of things are stopping us from doing what we will. I propose that we do a tarot spread.

Some people will feel uneasy about doing this. Some may feel silly, forgetting, of course, that by this point in my book they have visited an oracle, killed their bosses, painted themselves red, scryed, wore silk pajamas, and had a wonderful time doing it. Silliness is fun. Fun is good.

Others, and this is more serious, because of religious or other forms of constipation, are fearful of using something "occult." Role-playing and visualization are one thing, but tarot cards! Well, if you can't bring yourself to do this, save your immortal soul and go have a cup of coffee. Come back later. We'll be doing a space walk then. It will be fun and I won't laugh at you.

Actually, we are not really going to use the cards themselves. What we will be doing is a mental visualization using a tarot spread as our format. The reason we will not be using the cards is that they have a concrete format and very specific types of pictures on them. I want to free your imagination in this book rather than limit it. So for this exercise, the images on your cards will be entirely of your own making. I am only using a set format so as to give you something to hang your hat on, so to speak.

Okay, we need to use a fairly simple spread and one that includes the time elements and the idea of opposing forces in our lives.

A spread that fits these criteria is the Magic Seven-spread (see diagram). As its name indicates, seven cards are actually used in this spread. They are placed as follows:

Card one represents the past of the matter we are focusing on. Card two is the present and follows from the past (or card one). Card three, naturally, is the immediate future. It is a synthesis of the past and present; cards one and two. Card four represents the type of energy prevalent in the situation under consideration. It is the type or current of energy you must learn to use to master this situation. Card five is

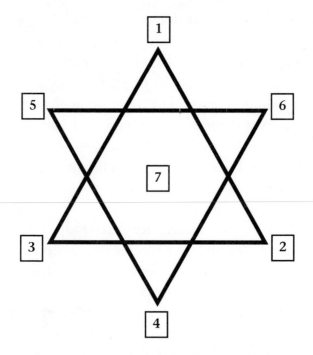

the surrounding environment, what is going on around this particular situation. Card six is of central importance for us in this exercise. It is the opposing force, what is stopping us, from achieving the possible future we have picked. Card seven is the result, if and when we have responded to the forces surrounding the situation.

Sometimes when doing tarot readings, a card is also chosen to represent the person or client asking the questions—actually instead of the "person asking the question," which as we have seen is a power position, we can also say that the querant is "the person pursuing the matter." It is somehow less limiting. At any rate, the card usually picked to represent the person pursuing the matter is a court card, knight, queen, prince, or princess. These are usually picked for their astrological affinities to the querant. Since we won't be using the actual deck, these options will not be available to us. Perhaps we can use something else.

Before we start, and so that we will understand where we are going and how what we are doing is similar to and different from an actual tarot reading, we need to discuss the tarot cards themselves.

The tarot deck is composed of seventy-eight cards. There are four suits: wands, cups, swords, and pentangles (or coins). Each suit starts with an ace and runs up to ten. There are forty number cards and sixteen court cards, which add up to fifty-six cards. The last twenty-two cards of the seventy-eight are called the Trumps. These cards are very specific in their symbolism. They refer to the twenty-two paths of the Tree of Life. They are the twenty-two fixed connections between the ten interpenetrating spheres of the universe. If you want, you could conceive of the Trumps as cosmic plumbing. They are pipes carrying energy from the valves and cauldrons of the cosmos. When you deal the Trumps, you are therefore not dealing cards, but dealing paths of energy.

Now that I've given away my next book, we can go on with our own reading. How do you feel right now? Are you optimistic? Apprehensive? Why do you feel that way? What forces or people in your life are making you feel this way? Look out the window. Heave a sigh. Snap your eyes closed! What do you see? I usually tell you to have a note pad with you, but not this time. For this exercise, we are going to let out minds "morph." The psychic pictures themselves are going to be our raw material.

Hold what you have just seen in your mind. Bet you can't, but do your best. Place yourself in the picture if you are not already there. How do you look? How do you want to look? How do you feel that you look? Try to combine these three images into one and place it somewhere in the first picture you had when you closed your eyes. Can you do it? It's almost like the sand painting they do in Tibet or in the American Southwest. A little breeze, a little disturbance, and the picture changes. This is how your mind works and as we've seen, your mind has a lot to do with how your world appears. Not too stable, is it?

169

The composite picture you now have is the card we'll use to represent you, the querant; the person pursuing the matter. Now think of something you want to happen in the future. Will it happen? Let's do the spread and see. We have to deal the first card, the past. Open your eyes again. What in the hell is your neighbor doing? Snap them shut. What do you see? This is the first card. The opening and closing of our eyes is the automatic shuffle. Let's pretend. Again, what do you see? What does this picture mean? How do you feel about it? Finally, do you see or feel any connections to your original card, the one representing you, the person pursuing the matter?

When you were just now thinking about the querant card and your past card, did your past card change? Is it changing now? Sand painting again, right? Well, try real hard to hold these two cards as they are.

Now we want to deal card number two, the present. Again we open our eyes, clear our brains, automatically shuffle, and slam our eyes shut. Same procedure. What do you see? How do you feel about it? Since the present is supposed to flow from the past, what connections do you see or feel? Are the sand grains from the past card and your querant card flowing into the present? Well, that's no good! Try to hold these pictures separate. Do the best you can.

Let's do one more and then we can recap the first three time-dimension cards as they relate to each other and you, the person pursuing the matter. Do the drill. Open your eyes, shuffle your brain, close your eyes, and deal the immediate future card. Whoa! What's this baby like? What do you see? What colors? What images? How do you feel? This card is supposed to be the synthesis of the past and the present and, of course, you as the querant are included in here too. Do you see all of these elements? Is the sand again blowing from the other cards? Can you really stop them or are the other cards fading as the card in front of you gets clearer and brighter? Try to keep every detail about all of these cards. You can't? Let me let you in on a little secret. That's what you're supposed to see. So far we've dealt with four pictures, four cards. In the space of just a few moments, even these pictures are fading. They are becoming nothing. This past is becoming! An odd thing to say. We only think of things becoming something in the future.

To help us understand the pictures we have just seen, we turn to the inverted triangle of cards, four, five, and six. Can you remember the positions of these cards from the diagram? It's okay, go ahead and turn back to it. Da da da. Get it now? Oh, by the way, can you remember the four cards we've just been using? Fuzzy, huh? A dirty trick my getting you to focus on the diagram, right? But again, it shows just how fragile the mind and, I might add, how fragile our current reality is. We are only dealing with seven cards. Eight if you add the querant, yourself, in this spread. What if we needed more, like in the Life Spread which uses all seventy-eight? Present reality is narrow because the mind is narrow. Everything beyond the closely drawn circle of the mind has again drifted into nothingness. Both past and future back into the realm of possibilities.

Card four is the type of energy you must master in order to respond to your situation. Open, shuffle, deal. What appears to you? Do you understand how this picture represents a type of energy? Think about it, any intuitive flashes? Can you tell yourself what you need to encounter and use in order to bring about the result you want? Again, how does this make you feel? Why do you feel this way? Finally, can you still make out some of your previous cards? If you can, can you see this energy moving through these cards? Does it connect them to each other and if so, how? If this energy runs through all of the other cards, does it meld them all together into a picture? If it does, time, you must realize by now, is gone and there is this one *dharma* and, nothingness.

We pull back. The environment in which you must work. Card five. Hold card four if you can. Shuffle, close, do you see the energy of card four exploding into the environment? Chips of fire into the *dharmic* sky. Forming images as they coalesce. Another picture is forming—card five. What is it? What's in it? Is the energy still there? Can you still see it? Describe it in this picture. Stay in the darkness. This picture too will fade like the sparks in a fireworks display as they burn out. Take one falling spark, energize it, pull it out into the sky and let it expand. It is a picture of the forces that oppose you and the future you want. They are made of fire, luminous, lighting up the whole sky. Card six. How do you feel? Do you recognize these forces or, these people? What and who are they? How are they working against you? Activate them, make them show you how they plan to block you. Watch this picture as long as you can. Hold it as long as you can.

You couldn't hold this picture without other thoughts and images intervening for even a moment, could you? Neither can the forces seen in that picture hold together in just that precise combination for much longer. The forces disentangle and that picture, that conjunction, becomes like all else, every other *dharma*, nothingness.

What is opposing you? Nothing, you can honestly tell yourself.

How do you think we get to card seven, the result? We get there because nothing stops us from getting there. The images, all of those bright and flickering images from the querant card, yourself and the image you had of yourself, through the full line of time, acted on by forces and events, all of these pictures were the process, not individual things. Just as with every other action, event, force—or *dharma*—in the world, they flow into each other, leaving nothing and collapsing into the result. What do you honestly see surrounding the result? Nothing. All *dharmas* are like this; there is the result, a picture or image changing just like the movie image we used earlier to explain *dharmas* and nothingness.

I said earlier that there are many kinds of nothingness. In

fact, there is even a list of the various nothings developed by an Irish philosopher, Johannes Scotus Eriugena (Right, a dead Irishman; if such a thing is possible) in the ninth century.

While Europe was in the deepest pit of the Dark Ages—raping, pillaging, slaughtering, annoying farm animals—the Irish monks, off on their stone in the Atlantic, and as yet undiscovered by our friends the Vikings, managed to keep European civilization and thought alive. They read not only Latin, but managed to preserve the Greek language, and with it, Greek thought. It is from this environment that John the Scot, a wildly original thinker, drew.

While the Latin of his name is Johannes Scotus Eriugena, it is translated as John the Scot. An anomaly; in the ninth century, "Scotus" meant "Irishman," and, the last word "Eriugena" also meant Irishman. So although his name is John the Scot, Scotus Eriugena was Irish.

We won't go into John's life except to say that he left Ireland in about 843 to become a scholar at the Court of Charles the Bald in France. At dinner one night, the king asked him, "What separates a Scot from a sot?" John supposedly quipped, "Just the table, My Lord." John was a fun guy and as gutsy as all the rest of his countrymen.

Of importance to us are John's five categories of nothingness, or, as he calls them, "non-being." I can get into quite a fight with other students of philosophy over the difference between nothingness and non-being, but they're not writing this book so I can blur the differences for our practical purposes.

To understand John the Scot, we have to understand his starting point: Nature. To John, nature included all that is and, all that is is not. The terms "being" and "non-being" are relative terms only. The being of one thing is the non-being of its opposite. A stupid example: Red is "not blue." If red exists at any given place and time, blue does not exist. Blue, therefore, is non-existent. Nothing, at this place and time. How much blue is there? None. But conversely, if the color blue should exist at a certain place and time, then red is our non-existent being.

Of course, in fairness, you can say, well, blue or red are not nothing. Just because they are not before me right now doesn't mean they don't exist. Oh yeah? I put a red ball in front of you. Show me the blue. Well, I know what blue is, you say. Oh yeah, well I know what a unicorn is. Show me one. Now listen, George, I've seen blue before, you say. Okay, where is it now? Why, er, in my mind. Oh, well that's where my unicorn is. It won't do to punt and say that you have an idea of what blue is, because I also have an idea of what a unicorn is. Nor will it do to say you know what blue is, because I also know and so do you, for that matter, what a unicorn is. But you can argue, blue is possible, unicorns are not. Oh? So you know all of the possibilities in the entire universe? An infinity inside an infinity. Wow! You're pretty smart!

The point is that John the Scot, ten centuries before Jean-Paul Sartre, hit upon a truth that goes even beyond that of the modern Frenchman: The concepts of being and nothingness are relative to each other. The one term is meaningless without the other, and, therefore, neither term has any absolute meaning. The being of one thing is the non-being of another. Being itself is a predicate that does not imply anything other than a relationship with its opposite. To say that a big screen TV exists in my living room does not say that a bookcase in my bedroom doesn't exist. It is only to say that the bookcase is not here now. "Here and now and not something else" is the meaning of existence. Existence, what is, only makes sense as a string of relative terms. There is nothing, therefore, that exists absolutely, and, conversely, nothing that does not exist absolutely. "Being and non-being" are one concept. And this is the point where John the Scot started whiling away his afternoons at the court of Charles the Bald waiting for supper.

Since philosophers generally tend to divide existence into categories, and since "non-being," nothing, was as "real" and necessary as what passed for being or reality at any moment, John thought it only fair to categorize non-being.

The first category of non-being, nothing, is that which escapes our senses and is beyond our intellect. An example John gives is God. We can't see Him or Her or understand Him or Her. For us, therefore, God does not exist and is nothing.

Second, like our example of red and blue, if we affirm one thing, that is, say it exists, we negate its opposite.

Third, potential being, something that can be, is the non-being of what it will eventually become. This is a fancy way of saying that before (and after) something is actually in front of us, it does not exist for us. It is nothing.

Fourth, things that begin and end are not real in comparison with things that never change and always exist. Actually, this seems to be a subcategory of non-being number one since we really have no experience, empirically or even intellectually (our minds, as we saw in the tarot exercise, are unstable and constantly changing) of such a being. God is the only possible "thing" in this category.

Finally, John, a Catholic monk, says that a human being exists as long as he or she has the image of God in him or her but ceases to exist when he or she sins and loses that image. This, however, seems to be a subcategory of category two. If you are sinless, sin is not here now. If you sin, sinlessness is gone.

There is a lot more to this discussion of non-being, non-existence, nothingness, the void, but I've already gotten too stuffy for this book. If you buy me a bottle of Jamesons, I'll stay up all night with you and we can get the rest of this straight. The unspoken premise of John's list is that both being and nothingness are relative not only to each other, but also to us. We cannot see or understand God. We cannot see or think two things at once. We have a limited perceptual and temporal field. The being and nothingness we talk about are only a type or style of being or nothingness unique only to human beings. Are there other types of being? Are there other types of nothingness? Who knows?

This relativism is also precisely the point where we came in. When the Buddha sought enlightenment twenty-five-odd centuries ago, the first thing he found was that nothing (that word again) was absolute and everything was relative. It was from this relativity that his enlightenment proceeded. What is the world made of? Blobs of experience. What is here and now and, what is not here and now. The here and now, however, is always ahead of and behind itself. It is constantly slipping into nothingness, and as Sartre showed, any attempt to point your finger and say "There it is!" is always occurring just one instant after our little blob of experience slips past us. All we are left with then, is our own actions. The world is made of energies and forces. We are just a subset of them.

The mistake, however, that we Westerners tend to make when faced with these realizations (and experiences, since all traditional yogic practices as well as what we've been doing with our exercises in this book make this point) is to see this as negative and depressing. But "negative" and depressing are not the same things. We've seen that negativity, the power to say "no," creates freedom. Freedom can be joined to the world as it is to make it a work of art. Since so much of the world is nothingness, unconditioned *dharmas*, literally nothing is stopping us from entering the Openings that life offers us and rolling in the infinity of possibilities that time continually dumps at our feet.

When I was young in Newport, Pennsylvania my mother would get our meat from the butcher and then take it home and grind it herself. She had an old iron crank meat grinder that she clamped to the table. Into the top she forced the hunks of beef and pork (we're Eastern European) and out of the front, into her waiting bowl poured strand after strand of ground meat. The image I get of time is of a cosmic meat grinder cranking out endless strands of possibilities. The possibilities are the meat of our lives and are there for us to take up and make something of.

We've learned how to move into the openings, the unconditioned space in our lives. We've learned to gather and use our energy there. We've met our irrationalities, our feelings, and our intuition. They have proven themselves to be experienced and trustworthy guides. They have shown us how to act and we have acted as they have shown. We know that the world is mostly unconditioned and that our *dharma* is truly our *dharma*. Our work of art. Since the unconditioned *dharma* is an opening into nothingness, we see clearly that nothing is stopping us. Our problems, those that we said at the beginning were unsolvable, are seen to themselves be slipping constantly into this unconditioned space. This space is ours and we swallow our problems, not the other way around. They have no power.

I want to do one more thing with you in parting. I'll share one of my personal visions with you. It probably means nothing, but that's what it's all about, right? We'll go together.

We left earth one hundred million light years, or, one second, ago. We have traveled inside of a space ship made of a metal that is very thin, but so strong that while the difference between inside and outside is practically non-existent, the integrity of our craft is inviolable. We will remain intact even in the face of the asteroid monsoons between Mars and Jupiter and the bursts of ray showers beyond Alpha Centauri.

We move near the speed of light further and deeper into violet space, but we never find emptiness. There are great voids, and there are massive clouds of shimmering dust, but nowhere is there emptiness.

Beyond a galaxy-wide coil of neon light, there is a glass

station. It sits suspended there, needing no support because it is surrounded by the void of space. The shape is haphazard. Incomprehensible. Almost accidental. Still, it betrays design.

We slow and drift. Engines dead and quiet. We enter a crystal tube, luminous reds and blues and lavenders spilling across the surface, waves of energy activating the tube in which our ship comes to rest.

We leave the airlock and find ourselves somewhere in the massive bowels of the crystal station. There is a faint, almost imperceptible sound. A clinking; a tinkling. Aren't we alone? Fear spreads through our bodies like poison or a narcotic. We must find the source of this sound! We must know what we are facing!

We frantically search the monstrous station. We know, however, just from a glance, that it is so large that we could never search every part of it in many life times. But we are afraid, and we search everywhere. Even though it is glass and quite transparent, we just cannot accept the fact that we see everything. We still hear the sound. The faint, irritating sound!

We drag ourselves from enclosure to enclosure. Stars explode into sunsets and sunrises and nebula and dwarfs expand and contract. We will not look. We are very, very busy. Our survival depends on our finding the source of this irritating sound.

We are finally thoroughly exhausted. We are stuck in a small room and cannot breathe. We glance around through the transparent glass as a double star explodes its light over the light years from the edge of the universe. We cannot find the sound and the beauty of the double star has calmed us. We pass through a diamond door and find ourselves standing on a flat, oblong, irregularly shaped platform that juts out into infinite space. We walk slowly and calmly toward the edge. Our breath slows as we are bathed in the unnamed colors of the exploding stars. A solar wind rises and gently and warmly passes by our faces.

And then we hear the sound again. This time it is much closer. Now, however, it sounds like music. Soft, clear music. Random, but still music. It sounds—Asian.

We look up in the direction of the sound. Overhead is a rod of glass extending into space from the walls of the station. On the end of the rod, suspended by an almost invisible nylon strand, is a wind chime. It is a wind chime of geometrical shapes of flat glass, suspended to catch the movements of the cosmic winds. Our mouths hang open. Then we laugh. Our laughter flies away and is lost somewhere beyond our sight. We gaze back at the double star.

I must return now. I have my own things to do. You may stay as long as you like.